Broken Vessels

Finding Wholeness, Freedom, and Purpose

JUDY TABER

ISBN: 978-1-66788-668-8 (softcover)
ISBN: 978-1-66788-669-5 (eBook)

Dedications

I am so grateful for the people in my life who have blessed me in countless ways. You've co-labored with Jesus on his restorative work in my life, and for that, I give thanks and praise to God for the mercy and grace I have received from him through each of you.

First, to my son, Doug, "But many who are first will be last, and last first" (Matt 19:30). Though you may not be the firstborn, you are the first in my thanksgiving. Thank you for sticking with me and never giving up on me.

To my daughter, Charla, I hope that you will find the answers you need to understand why I was so difficult to live with. I pray that you will find peace in your heart when you think of me. Even with all that has happened, I am so very proud of you.

To Chuck and Meg Kraft, saying thank you is not enough for all you have meant to me. Thank you for seeing me through Jesus' eyes and teaching me to see myself by the same means. Thank you for helping me understand what it means to be partnered with Jesus, yoked together with him co-laboring in the work of his Kingdom. May this book bless you and honor you for all your devotion to Jesus and partnering with him in setting the captives free.

To Pastors Bubba and Melany Justice, you've taught me what it means to have a pastor's heart as you've poured out so much of your life into me. You've taught me how to love the poorest of the poor. I will always be grateful for all you've done for me.

To Kathy Holder, you are one of the hidden secrets in the church, a gem that no one knows about except Jesus and those that you bless. And you have blessed me immeasurably. Thank you for always being available to me physically, financially, and prayerfully.

To Richard and Karen Soikkeli, I cannot express enough my gratitude for your prayers and partnership in this ministry. I appreciate everything you've done to stand with me through all my troubles.

To Tamra and the Breeden family, although you have moved to heaven, you taught me to walk the walk with unwavering faith. You showed me how to keep my eyes focused on Jesus without questioning the path He directs me to take. I love you all dearly.

Thank you to everyone who has supported Hearts Set Free financially and prayerfully. You have co-labored with me in binding the brokenhearted and setting captives free. May all of you be blessed for the kindness you have shown me and this ministry.

Lastly, thanks to Bob Morita, without whom this book would not have been written. Thank you for believing in the mission of Hearts Set Free and partnering with me in this ministry.

Note regarding front cover image[1]

---

1 Special thanks to Andrea from Kintsugi Décor (www.kintsugidecor.com) whose work inspired the image on the front cover. Kintsugi is a Japanese centuries old technique of repairing ceramics. In the hands of the master, broken pieces are melded back into wholeness where in the repaired articular is even more beautiful and unique than the original..

Forward

Elgie "Bubba" Justice
Chief Financial Officer and Missions Coordinator
Vineyard, USA

JUDY TABER IS A GIFT OF GOD TO THE BODY OF CHRIST. I HAVE known and worked with Judy for over 20 years. This book gives the readers the in-depth background that equipped Judy to be the teacher and minister she is today.

When I first met Judy, I was somewhat skeptical of her approach to dealing with demonic and inner healing. I was invited to a prayer session with Judy. In our time together, Judy asked the Holy Spirit to bring to memory anything that He wanted to deal with. I immediately saw a picture in my mind of me sitting amid pornographic material. I had been exposed to pornography for the first time as a seven-year-old boy. Later my mother married a man who had many pornographic magazines that were accessible. We had access to pornographic movie channels. Even though I was a Christian, I was addicted to pornography.

As a young adult, I was delivered from the demonic power behind pornography, and I thought that was the end. As Judy prayed for me and I relayed the picture of me sitting amid pornography, Judy asked, "Where is Jesus?" I expected that Jesus would either be angry with me or he would be sad and disappointed with me. Instead, as I watched the picture unfold in my mind, Jesus took a white cloth and covered over the pornography. 1 Peter 4:8 immediately came to mind: "love covers a multitude of sins." At that moment, I experienced healing from the shame of pornography and became an advocate for Judy to whoever will listen.

I eventually brought Judy on staff at the Inverness Vineyard Church. She traveled with me to Africa, and God used her powerfully to minister to people from different tribal and racial backgrounds.

I wholeheartedly recommend this book and the ministry of Judy Taber to everyone.

Prologue

MY LIFE HAS BEEN AN ARDUOUS JOURNEY. BUT FOR MOST OF MY life, I did not know that it was. That may sound strange, and it will seem even stranger after you read through this book, especially the first few chapters. I did not have a typical childhood or adolescence, but growing up, I never realized that my life was not normal or typical. I recognize now that I suffered through a lot of traumas, some of which are probably within the normal range of childhood experiences, but many of them were not. I had faced issues of abandonment, rejection, and unworthiness. I carried the responsibility of protecting and, to a certain degree, parenting my younger siblings while I was still a child myself. My parents were very irresponsible, and on many occasions, I was forced to deal with debt collectors, covering (i.e., lying, making excuses, etc.) for my parents. We struggled financially and moved from one location to another just ahead of the debt collectors. I can't tell you how many schools I attended growing up.

Folks would also say how mature I was even before I was a teenager. I had to be, but all that responsibility was beyond my ability to carry. I didn't know how much stress carrying my family's burdens was causing me until I became a parent. As my children grew from infants to toddlers and into their adolescent years, my memories and emotions bubbled up and dominated my thoughts. Different stages in their lives brought back memories of my childhood difficulties and at times erupted into painful emotional episodes. Although I was aware of the emotions stemming from these memories, I could not control the effect they had on my behavior. I became maniacally obsessed with protecting and controlling my children and my husband. I was unable to control my compulsion. I cannot tell you the clinical definition of my emotional state, but I know that it manifested into a nervous disorder (that I will describe in detail later). Beyond that, I can tell you that I had an enormous amount of anger bottled up and a self-loathing that resulted in a destructive pattern of behavior directed mostly toward myself, but there was a spillover directed toward my family, most pointedly toward my mother.

But, thanks to Jesus, my story doesn't end there. I write to describe how Jesus healed me, and he continues to bring even deeper levels of healing to me even today. I know that the transformation that has happened deep within my heart is nothing short of a miracle. The joy and peace I have in my heart today are beyond what I thought were possible for most of my life. I am writing this book because I know that this miraculous transformation is available to everyone.

For some of you, the first half of this book will be heavy. I do not know how to communicate the depth of God's grace without showing you the depth of the pit he lifted me out of. If you struggle through the first half of the book, ask the Holy Spirit to help you bear through it. I want to assure you that it turns around miraculously. The first half of this book is about me, Judy Taber, and clearly points to the direction my life was headed. It is not pretty and would not have ended well. The second half of this book is about Jesus and His supernatural work of redemption and resurrection. My hope is that through your reading you will be inspired to seek the Holy Spirit to provide you with the same "new life" I experienced so that you obtain the same joy and peace I have from being in unity with Jesus.

I've tried to be careful with the words I use in this book because I know that there are some "trigger" words that can shut people down. For some, the words "inner healing" can be a showstopper. Please do not let it. I use the words "inner healing" and "deep healing" interchangeably. Both terms or phrases simply mean "transformation" of the inner person, soul or heart. The apostle Paul describes this in 2 Cor 4:16–17 (NIV): "[16] Therefore we do not lose heart. Though outwardly we are wasting away, yet inwardly we are being renewed day by day. [17] For our light and momentary troubles are achieving for us an eternal glory that far outweighs them all."

Earlier in the same letter to the church in Corinth, Paul says that we are being transformed into his likeness or image (2 Cor 3:18). Since our outer body continues to "waste away" day by day, year by year, it is not our body that is being renewed. It is the inner person—our heart or soul (mind, will, and emotions) —that is being transformed day by day, but only as we look upon Jesus with unveiled hearts (that is, without masks). That is what I am referring to when I write about "inner healing" or "deep healing."

Depending upon your denominational upbringing, some may read this as "psychobabble." I want to say that I respect the science of psychology and have done ministry with and for many friends and associates in the field of psychology. I do not mean to disparage, by any means, the work of psychologists, especially those who balance the spiritual needs of folks with the emotional. In my writings, I hope that I do not offend my friends and associates within this field. Those who put "inner or deep healing" in their "psychobabble" bucket will likely be offended by some things contained herein. I hope that you are willing to give me some grace and will continue to read through to the end. The type of transformation I desire and continue to experience is the type that changes you from the inside and molds you into the image of Jesus rather than public figures who are idolized by the world. This type of change on the inside results in our being able to forgive those who persecute us. It gives us the ability to love our neighbor and even our enemies. It gives us the ability to turn the other cheek. This type of transformation goes far beyond anything that psychology alone can hope to attain. It is the type of change that enables you to be set free from the bondages of all your emotional pain and traumas and live a life full of peace and joy in the midst of trials and tribulations. This transformation is a holy, God-breathed freedom that allows you to be in the world but not of the world. Most importantly, it gives you the ability to love yourself in the same manner that Jesus loves you: unconditionally.

This book is about spiritual warfare. It deals with the invisible war that affects all of us. Through scripture and my own experiences, I have learned much about the tactics of our enemy. I will speak freely about the demonic influences in my life and how, by the authority given to me by Jesus, I have been able to live victoriously. Sadly, although there is much content, biblically speaking, in regard to angels, demons, and spiritual warfare, there are those that refuse to acknowledge the reality of the invisible realm. Again, I ask for indulgence for those folks who do not want to read or hear about demonic influence, especially on believers in Jesus Christ. There is too much at stake for me not to speak upon this critical aspect of living in the fullness of life that Jesus desires to impart upon us. I have learned that we must be engaged in spiritual warfare to be set free and that this war is more than just a defensive battle. I recognize that we must also be on the offensive—the gates of Hades shall not prevail (Matt. 16:18). I believe that God has commissioned us to go on a spiritual offensive to open blind eyes, preach the good news, and set the captives free (Isa. 61:1–2, Luke 4:16–20, Matt. 28:18–20). My mission, that is, my purpose for living (and I hope you will join me in this mission), is to be partnered with God and extend His Kingdom by making disciples from all nations. It is a Kingdom characterized by his unconditional love, acceptance, and forgiveness and expressed through his disciples.

Lastly, I want to tell you a bit about the title of this book. God created us in his likeness and to do good works (Eph 2:10). Multiple scripture verses use vessels (clay pots or jars) as a metaphor for humanity. We are supposed to be containers for His Holy Spirit to be poured into so that we can be used by God as vessels for His Holy Spirit to be poured out of and into others. But we are all broken vessels and cannot repair ourselves. It is only through the work of Jesus that we can be healed so that we can be effectively used by Him. Without that miraculous healing work by Jesus, we are nothing more than a leaky sieve, and for all our good intentions, nothing of eternal value is gained.

The freedom that I write about is not freedom from political oppression, nor is it about our rights (as most Americans think of freedom as legally guaranteed through the US Constitution). It is not freedom from the chaos resulting from the various tragedies that everyone experiences in life. It is a freedom that comes from dwelling in Christ. It is the freedom that comes from our choosing to live by His Spirit and not by the path dictated to us by the world culture we live in. It is the freedom to live victoriously regardless of the circumstances of life.

Finally, my hope is that you will find your purpose for living. I believe that everyone who has said "yes" to Jesus and chooses to live by His Spirit has a calling on their life. Your calling is unique to you. It is your specific, God-given purpose for living. It is shaped not only by your innate talents and skills but also by God's spiritual gifts you receive and by your unique life situations and experiences. But your calling cannot be understood or expressed appropriately until you have been made whole (i.e., healed or transformed in the inner person) and you've experienced the freedom that comes from being in unity with Jesus.

Introduction

by Robert Morita

2 Timothy 2:20–21

> [20]A large house contains not only vessels of gold and silver, but also of wood and clay. Some indeed are for honorable use, but others are for common use. [21]So if anyone cleanses himself of what is unfit, he will be a vessel for honor: sanctified, useful to the Master, and prepared for every good work.

AFTER I HAD AGREED TO HELP JUDY WITH HER STORY, WE HAD a few things that needed to be worked out. I think the biggest issue was agreeing upon the book title. My desire was to call it "A Broken but Noble Vessel," and after you have read her story, the "Broken" part will be obvious. "Noble" is a word that Judy, in her humility, struggled with. While that is not at all how she sees herself, it is how I see Judy. I did not know Judy during the period prior to the healing work of Jesus in her life. What I have witnessed is a self-sacrificing woman who has been "sanctified" and is serving her Lord as a noble vessel.

Judy Taber's story is one that must be told. It is the story of a partnership between Jesus and a woman who had been broken and left in life's dumpster. Her tale is not intended for anyone who is a successful self-made man or woman who has no need for God. If you are unwilling to accept Jesus' path of humility, then there is no need for you to read any further. If you have never suffered in life or wondered why God allows people to suffer, then you will not benefit from reading this book. This is not an American "rags to riches" success story. This is a story of Jesus' redemptive power for anyone who is willing to say "Lord, use me in all my brokenness for the glory of your Kingdom." It is a story of deep healing, the transformative work of God available to anyone who desires to be set free from the bondages of a mindset hardened by life in an oppressive, abusive, and fallen world. Judy does not have lofty credentials; she doesn't have a title or a three-letter acronym following her name. She is not famous. Yet God has chosen Judy to operate with Kingdom authority to transform the hearts of men and women across North America, Europe, Asia, Africa, and more than a dozen different nations therein.

Judy is familiar with suffering. I would not wish her life for myself or my loved ones, but through her brokenness, I see God in His unconditional, yet at times offensive, love. Some of her suffering has come through life's circumstances and not through any choices of her own. In this aspect, she is like Job. Life is not fair, and sometimes, through no fault of our own, we fall victim to events beyond our control.

Some of her suffering has come from her own decisions, made without Godly wisdom and Holy Spirit inspiration. Even though Judy had been saved in her early childhood and knew the scriptures, she did not know how to hear and be dependent upon the Holy Spirit's guidance. In this way, perhaps she is like many Americans who grow up in a Christian family and attend church. Salvation comes early, but without learning how to hear the voice of the Holy Spirit, we understand God to be like a genie in a bottle, someone we let out and ask for help from when we need it. We can read the Bible, but instead of being inspired by the Holy Spirit for understanding, we read into it selectively, reading only what we want to hear and see to validate what we already know or have been taught. Unfortunately, many Christians have not learned how to hear God's voice or how to test every spirit, so the god of this world is still firmly seated in place, controlling, deceiving, and holding captive their minds and hearts.

Sadly, some of her suffering has come from the hands of Christian church members filled with a religious spirit. Like Job's friends, a narrow religious theology, especially regarding suffering, leads to hardness of heart and will eliminate you from being used for God's noble purposes.

The author of Hebrews tells us to "set our eyes upon Jesus, the author and perfecter of our faith" (Heb 12:2). In doing so, we may forget that Jesus is the suffering servant. In the midst of our pain, we often look to Him to take away our suffering, but we may not realize that it is through the suffering that our faith is perfected. Judy has had to drink from Jesus' cup of suffering, but in doing so, she has been filled with His joy and the hope that His finished work has yet to come for her, for her family, and for her friends.

Judy is not the perfect person "living the dream." Even to this day, with all the deep healing and deliverance she has experienced, she suffers from physical ailments and financially lives month to month. On top of all her crushing life events, God has given her the gift of burden bearing. She empathizes with the folks she prays for to the extent that she feels their pain and sorrows. As God has chosen her to be used for his noble purposes, she has learned to yield to His Holy Spirit and is empowered to bring down the strongholds of the enemy not by her own knowledge and strength but by the Spirit's leading and by His authority. She has become a holy warrior for God, fighting against the lies of demonic spirits oppressing those whose desire is to be set free.

If you decide to read her story, then you should be aware that the spirits of shame are likely to be aroused if shame is present in your life. If you have been in church and recognize that you've been doing church instead of being the church, you should be aware that religious spirits are likely to be aroused in you. Judy frankly discusses the effect of demons in her life, and for some, that may be highly offensive. This is not a "the devil made me do it" book. It treats the reality of the invisible domain of God, Jesus, the Holy Spirit, demons, and angels in a practical and illustrative manner. It is fundamentally a book describing spiritual warfare from the perspective of someone who has been on the front lines. As you read Judy's stories, some of them may be difficult to believe, and that is ok. My education, training, and vocation were in engineering, so if I did not know Judy personally or had not been involved in her ministry, I would have a hard time believing them myself. But if you keep an open mind and ask God for new revelations, I believe He will open the eyes of your heart to see into the invisible realm with more wisdom and understanding.

This book is not about glorifying Judy; that would be the last thing she would want. It is intended to provoke inward and upward thought and can be used in a group reading with conversation that is intended to deepen your relationship with God. As such, each chapter concludes with a section called "Reflections of the Heart"—a series of questions and/or comments to help focus your thoughts upon God and your own heart. If you have additional questions or would like prayer, additional resources are available to you through the Hearts Set Free website[2].

One final introductory note: As you read through Judy's story and reflect on your own life, my hope is that you will seek to discover God's noble purpose for you. Your story is part of His grand masterpiece, woven together in the ensemble of a diverse chorus made up of people from every tribe, tongue, and nation. That masterpiece is yet to be finished, and your role is still to be played out. I pray that the Holy Spirit will bless you through Judy's story, and that, like Judy, His redemptive power will resurrect you from your brokenness, give you a new identity in Him, and set you apart for his noble purposes. And in Him, may you be filled to his fullness with joy, peace, and contentment in everything that you do.

---

2 https://www.heartssetfree.org/

Table of Contents

Chapter 1

Have you met my demons?

WHEN DR. CHARLES KRAFT ASKED ME TO WRITE ABOUT MY experience with "inner healing" (or "deep healing") and "spiritual warfare" in reference to demonization, I didn't have to hesitate when giving him an answer. Yes was the only answer available to me. If what I share helps just one person be set free from the captivity of the enemy, then I share this testimony with a humble, joyful heart, giving all the glory and thanksgiving to my Father, God. If you had asked me before my experience with inner healing and deliverance through ministry with Dr. Kraft, "Do you believe a Christian could be demonized?" my answer would have been, "A Christian cannot be demonized because the Holy Spirit lives in him/her and where He dwells, evil has to flee." If this sounds familiar, it's because that is the traditional teaching in many western Christian theologies. But if I were to be asked today the same question, I would answer, "What better place for demons to hide than behind a theology that teaches that Christians cannot be demonized?" Based upon my own experiences and study of scripture, I do believe a Christian can be demonized (but not demon-possessed; see Appendix A: Can Christians be demonized?). I believe this has been a strategy used by our enemy to keep "Christians" like myself deceived.

Some of the negative emotions, habits, and actions we experience in our lives are not caused only by sin, but sometimes there is demonic influence that causes us to respond to adverse situations in a negative, sinful way.

We sin when we align ourselves with demons by choosing to become bitter, unforgiving, and resentful. In contrast, when we make the decision to be victorious over these situations, extending God's unconditional love and forgiveness to those who have hurt us deeply, we align ourselves to God, and His peace and joy restore our soul. This does not mean that we agree with what has been done to us, but we choose not to allow our enemy to use these situations to destroy our self-esteem and, many times, our very lives. We forgive when we give up our right to judgment and revenge and give the perpetrator over to Jesus for his righteous judgment. Sometimes that forgiveness is a moment-by-moment battle that must be waged daily (70 times 7).

I don't believe every problem is demonic. In our Western-based theology, we tend to believe in the extremes. Either demons are extremely powerful and all our problems are demonic, or Christians can't be demonized. I have come to believe that good things and bad things happen in life regardless of our standing before God. "He causes His sun to rise on the evil and the good, and sends rain on the righteous and the unrighteous" (Matthew 5:45b).

We all have problems, but it's how we respond to the problem that either leads to a victorious life filled with inner peace and joy or defeat—enslaved to anger, bitterness, or depression. I would just like to offer a possibility for you to consider: when you cannot get a victory in particular areas of your life, then perhaps there is a demonic influence. As I begin to tell you how my life has been changed through inner healing and deliverance, I want to say that it has only been through the grace, mercy, and unconditional love of my Father God that I have been able to receive a supernatural healing in my wounded heart.

I would like to acknowledge that I have received much grace from my children, whom I raised through all my brokenness. I had a heart of bitterness, resentment, and unforgiveness toward many people, even the people I loved the most. It takes a special person, yielded to the Holy Spirit, to be able to love someone like me. Although I may have looked good on the outside to those who only knew me superficially, I was broken on the inside.

I would like to emphasize this: the memories and emotions that I have are expressed through my eyes and my experience. I express these as I have perceived them through the lens of my own suffering. In no way do I want to bring condemnation or express a judgmental attitude toward any of the people I mention. It is not my place to judge their motives or actions. Only God has that right. When referring to the hurt caused by my parents, I have to say they were two broken people raising a daughter the best they knew how to. I have never thought or believed my parents didn't love me. I don't think they ever realized how deeply their actions hurt me.

In place of judgment, I offer the Father's unconditional love and forgiveness to anyone and everyone that I have had a relationship with. My motivation for writing this is only to speak forth words of truth in relation to inner healing or deep healing of the soul. I pray that the words I write will be a testimony to the healing power of Jesus, which is available to all of God's children. But it is only available for those who ask Him and are willing to work with Him for their healing. May these words give you strength to step out in faith, trusting in Jesus to open the door of your wounded heart. May you allow the Holy Spirit to heal your deepest hurts, just as He has healed and continues to heal mine. I promise, Jesus will never let you down, and neither will the Holy Spirit cause you embarrassment. God always wraps His power in love. He is gentle and will not harm you. He will only extend the Father's love to you.

Reflections of the Heart

Although I have been a Christian since childhood, I never understood the authority and power available to me as His child in His Kingdom. My grandparents taught me that I was protected from any and all demonic attacks and influence. I never spent a moment pondering the tactics of our enemy and how his deception became a part of my thought processes, emotions, and behaviors.

As you read through these reflection questions, think about whether the enemy may have played a part in your life events, your spiritual and emotional well-being. Consider if it is possible that demonic spirits have misled you or the people who may have hurt you.

* * *

Are there people in your life presently who bring out the worst in you? Or do you experience outbursts of anger that come on suddenly with little or no reason—a situation in which something just came over you and you couldn't control your anger? Are there dates, names, sounds, sights, or smells that trigger a painful memory?

* * *

For most of my life, I denied that I was angry or that I held anger in my heart. I would say things like "I'm not angry, I'm just frustrated!" And as my voice grew louder, everyone else except me was able to see it. Until I could identify and acknowledge that I was angry, I could not be healed of it.

My good friend and mentor David DeBord taught me how to identify anger through a simple formula. He said you are angry if one or more of the following is true:

1. Carrying a hurt from the past
2. Frustration for the present
3. Fear of the future

If you've tried self-help books and counseling but still have lingering issues with emptiness and even depression and if inner peace and joy are evading you, then I invite you to let Jesus into your brokenness and bring His healing. Ask the Holy Spirit to show you the root of your pain, anger, or brokenness and give them to Jesus.

God heals our painful memories, but our memories continue to be part of our life history. We do not forget our difficult life events any more than Jesus does His own crucifixion. But now Jesus looks back at the cross and experiences the love and joy of the redemptive process. This is the goal of inner healing and deliverance.

Chapter 2

A flawed start on a good foundation

MY PARENTS ALWAYS STRUGGLED WITH THEIR FINANCES, AND it seems like we were always in debt. Since both my parents had to work and could not afford childcare, I lived a lot with my grandparents. I was always considered by them to be "their baby" or youngest child. They raised me as their child. They were "old-fashioned Pentecostal" ministers who believed in God and in the power of prayer. We lived in the church parsonage next door to the church my grandpa pastored. My grandpa would go to his church after lunch each day. There were days that I would lie in the grass outside his office door, playing in a clover patch. As I played, I always heard him crying out in prayer, asking God to protect his children and grandchildren. He would call each of our names out loud. After praying for his family, he would pray for every member of the church, their families, and any additional prayer needs. As a small child, I would find myself praying, asking God to hurry him up so he could play with me. I never realized that during these times, a hunger and love for prayer were being imparted to me. I picked up his mantel of prayer and the love for prayer for those God has laid on my heart.

I remember my grandparents praying over me, especially at night before bed when I was missing my parents. They would pray for peace and asked God to protect me, to keep His hand upon my life. God was faithful to their prayers. It has been evident all through my life, as you will see. God has protected me and continues to direct my path. I didn't know a lot about God, but I knew He was love and that only real love came from Him.

As I grew older, I was taught not to partake in the things of the world that were sinful and against God. I was taught to guard against the sins of the flesh so that I would be able to live a "life of holiness." I was taught to remember that God's word teaches us, "If a woman has long hair, it is a glory to her; for her hair is given to her for a covering" (1 Cor 11:14 NKJV). I will explain later why this verse is so pertinent to my life and to my path toward healing and freedom. I was taught that to love God is to honor Him and His word and that we must be servants for Him to all, especially those within His church.

However, I was never taught how to deal with the hurt and pain that people caused me, especially those I loved so dearly. I was taught to endure suffering quietly and without complaint. I was never taught how to process my emotions or discuss painful events. I don't remember anyone teaching or preaching John 14:30 (Amplified): "The prince (evil genius, ruler) of the world is coming. And he has no claim on Me—he has nothing in common with Me, there is nothing in Me that belongs to him, he has no power over Me." As a young child, I did not understand how to guard my heart against evil or how to keep the evil one from having a claim on me. I held a very simple belief that long hair was my covering. I never questioned what I was taught, and I retained their words of instruction within my heart.

I loved the time I was living with my grandparents, but I do have a few strong, painful memories that have stuck with me. The first memory I have is of a Sunday morning service when I was around four years old. I was told that I had to sing a solo accompanied by my aunt Sharon playing the piano. I did not want to participate, but with my grandma's persuasion (bribe), I agreed. I got about halfway through the song when I overheard two ladies in the second row laughing out loud and saying, "Oh, she is so cute but can't carry a tune!" I can distinctly remember how humiliated I felt! I stopped right then, crossed my arms, cried, and stomped away. I told my grandma I didn't want her gift (her bribe). I made a vow that I would never do this again. To this day, I still remember this experience every time I open my mouth to praise the Lord. Thankfully, through God's healing work in my heart, I have learned to laugh at the enemy trying to close my mouth again, and I sing louder!

The second painful memory is more devastating. My parents would come by for visits, typically over the weekend. At the end of the weekend, my parents would sneak off so that I wouldn't make a fuss. They would lie to me, telling me they weren't leaving, but they always did, and I would be crushed. I recognize now that these actions left me with abandoned issues later in life and with the inability to trust my parents in any capacity.

As our family grew, my parents had two additional children. It then became necessary for me to spend more time living at home with my family. In birth order, I am the firstborn of three children. There is a seven-and-a-half-year gap between me and my younger brother, Jene (the middle child), and a nine-year gap between me and my youngest brother, Jeff. Being the firstborn and only girl in my family, I found myself in the responsible position of "parenting" my younger siblings. Both of my parents had to work, so a lot of the childcare responsibility fell upon me, and I welcomed it with open arms. I don't remember being resentful of the responsibility, but I was no longer able to spend as much time with my grandparents as I would have liked. I went from being "Grandpa's little princess" to becoming an eight-year-old mother and maid, or so I felt.

When I was nine, my dad decided we should move to California so we could experience the "good life." At that time, my mother was pregnant with Jeff. Jene, the middle child, was always getting sick, requiring a lot of care from time to time. I remember that life was very difficult during that period of my life. My mother cried often, saying she wished she were dead and not pregnant. She didn't want another baby, and she wished he would die. I thought if she really felt this way about this unborn baby, she must feel the same way about Jene and me. I had a hard time understanding this since I was taught that a child was a gift from God.

It wasn't too many months after moving to Modesto that my mother gave birth to Jeff. Being a child myself, I never understood the mood swings due to the "baby blues." After coming home from the hospital with the baby, my mother was very disturbed emotionally. The very afternoon she came home, she became hysterical and took off walking. She said she was leaving and never coming back. I took my baby brother and held him in my arms, along with my brother, Jene. I promised them that they didn't have to worry. I would always be there to take care of them, even if Mom decided to never come home. Dad found her, but it took three days before he could convince her to come back. During this time, I took on the responsibility of "mothering" my brothers.

Things continued to get worse, and we soon moved to Los Angeles. Dad decided he wanted to live by the ocean and thought he could get a better job in L.A. We lived in a one-bedroom house that was falling apart, but it was clean. My mother always demanded a spotless home. Our home was located outside of the "Watts District" of L.A. This was during the late 60s, the time of the "Watts riots." The house had an enclosed front porch with a glass upper half. The porch was my bedroom. There was a bed, but no drapes or curtains. I would lay in my bed at night and see buildings burning from a distance. My dad was very prejudiced against black people. He continuously fed racial fear into my heart. The riots seem to validate and even amplify those fears.

When I was in the third grade (this was the third school I had attended that school year), there was this little black boy who sat next to me. He was so cute, and he asked me if I would be his friend. We would spend our recess together playing dodgeball. A few days later, my dad asked me how things were going at school, and I told him I had met a little boy who wanted me to be his friend. I told him he was black. The next day, my dad went to school and demanded that this little boy, my only friend, be moved to the other side of the classroom. My dad was loud and expressed his anger and prejudice without regret. I was so embarrassed by my dad's behavior. My dad didn't want any black person talking to me, much less sitting next to me. I was always very shy, and since we moved around a lot, it was very difficult to make friends. This was so unfair, and I knew it was wrong. At that moment, I purposed in my heart that I would never be a person given to prejudice.

Several months before school was out, my mother started to keep me home from school. She was working long, hard hours and couldn't afford childcare for my brothers, so the only choice was for me to stay home and care for them. I would keep the doors locked and the draperies closed. The school officials would send a social services person to check my house since I had been absent from school for so long. I was always terrified they would arrest my parents or, even worse, remove me and my brothers from our home.

My dad finally found a job and went to work for the Mattel Corporation. He was allowed to purchase toys at a discount, but even at a discount, we couldn't really afford them. One day, he brought home two new toys that he just had to have. One was an "Ouija Board," and the other was a "Magic 8 Ball." Dad really enjoyed playing with the "Ouija Board." He was always saying, "This thing really works. It answered my questions truthfully!" Or, so he thought. Dad's bringing these specific toys into our home had a detrimental spiritual significance that I will discuss later.

Things continued to get worse, and my parents decided it was time to move back home to Oklahoma. My aunt sent us enough money to get us home. So, my family, my cousin, and her baby—a total of three adults and four children (two of whom were toddlers)—piled into a two-door 57' Plymouth. Dad paid $250 for this car after his car was repossessed. No one thought we would make it 50 miles, much less all the way back to Oklahoma. We left in the middle of the night. I wasn't able to say goodbye to anyone. My parents hadn't paid rent or utilities in months, so the move was done furtively. We only took our clothes and left everything else behind. Unfortunately, this was the typical way we moved, which was also quite often.

When we arrived in Oklahoma, I went back to live with my grand-parents, and my family went to live with my dad's aunt. He didn't have a job, so he couldn't afford to rent a place to live. Since it was during the school year, they felt it was best for me to have a stable environment that would allow me to stay in the same school until they could establish a place of residency. This way, I wouldn't have to change schools two or three times in the same school year (which we had been doing). Living with my grand-parents was great except for the fact that I could not watch TV or be engaged in any "worldly" activities as I had become accustomed to doing while living with my parents. I did like the attention of being the "only child," except I felt extremely guilty because I promised my brothers that I would always be there to take care of them. I continuously worried about them, always fearing that something bad would happen to them. I worried that they weren't eating enough.

At the end of the first semester of my fifth grade school year, my parents made me come back home. I went from "princess" back to mother and maid. I don't question the fact that my parents loved me, but they were very immature as adults. They didn't love me the way my grandparents did or the way that Father God does.

It was during this time that I found myself not only being a "mom" to my siblings but also moving into the role of parenting my parents, a parental inversion in which I was trying to protect them from the consequences of their own irresponsibility. I became the person to answer the door when bill collectors showed up, explaining they weren't at home when, in reality, they were hiding in the closet or garage. I became the person who answered the phone, screening the calls to make sure they weren't from bill collectors. There were many excuses they gave me to tell people why they weren't available and that they would pay the bill, the rent, or the car payments. This created an internal conflict within me since I was taught to always tell the truth.

During this time, I became aware of a problem my dad was having. He was experiencing very severe migraine headaches. Dad had never been sick in all the years I could remember, but now he was having these terribly painful headaches. He would hold his hands over the top of his head and just scream with pain. He went to many doctors and was even hospitalized for treatment. They never seemed to find out what was causing them, and although he returned home with medication, it seldom helped him control the pain. These headaches continued for quite some time. They would quickly come and go. We weren't allowed to make any noise when Dad's head was hurting. It was my job to try to keep two highly active, loud little boys quiet, protecting them from Dad's anger.

I did not make a connection at that time, but there was a spiritual connection between the Ouija Board, the Magic 8 Ball, and my dad's headaches. The last time he was hospitalized for the headaches, my mom had me toss them into the garbage. She believed they were evil, and she wouldn't touch them. Within twenty-four to forty-eight hours after he returned from the hospital, the headaches vanished, even though the doctors had told us that Dad would have to live with the headaches.

Reflections of the Heart

I have found that some events, even in my early childhood, have had a profound effect on me in later life. Memory experts tell us that negative experiences and associated memories are "stored" in our mind more so than positive experiences. Although our memories are not entirely "correct," the more traumatic they are, they tend to be more accurate even in the details.

I recognize that in some of my more traumatic experiences, I made a vow or even cursed (myself or others). I have since learned that vows and curses are strongholds that demonic spirits can attach themselves to.

I also recognize that if I lack trust in my parents (or in other people who had authority over me), I can project those feelings to Father God without realizing I am doing so.

Regardless of whether you feel it or not, we live at the intersection between the material world and the invisible/spiritual world, which is beyond our ability to detect. But our activities in the material world do impact the invisible. Whenever we participate in activities such as the making of vows, oaths, curses, judgments, and condemnations or participate in occult-related activities (including channeling or being in submission to someone who channels spirit guides), we grant a "legal" right or access to demonic influences in our lives.

As you reflect upon the questions below, ask the Holy Spirit to show you anything that may have wounded you and/or may have derailed you from God's path and purpose for your life.

* * *

Reflect upon your early childhood. Are there any events that stick out in a negative manner? Have you ever cursed yourself or someone else or made a vow to do something or never to do something?

Do you have memories of people in authority over you (parents, teachers, childcare providers, etc.) who you feel you cannot trust or have abandoned you?

Perhaps you were brought up in a "religious" family (Christian or not) and experienced hypocrisy, legalism, self-righteousness, and judgmental and arrogant attitudes lacking love and tolerance.

Did you grow up in an environment friendly toward spiritual activity but lacking in Godly wisdom? This would include participating in activities involving games like the Ouija Board (inviting or channeling spirits) or being submitted to people who submitted themselves to spirit guides.

* * *

The good news is that Jesus Christ will set you free from any oppressive spirit that may have been granted a right to harass you. If you have not done so already, ask Jesus into your heart and submit to Him as your Lord and Savior. Then, whatever memory from your childhood comes up that is of a negative nature, simply invite Jesus into that memory and ask Him to set you free from any negative thoughts and emotions that still plague you. Renounce any oaths, vows, and/or dedications made to any spirit that is not of Jesus. Renounce any activities with ties to spiritualism. If you have held onto any bitterness, anger, or unforgiveness directed toward anyone, including yourself, give that person to Jesus and let Him be the judge. Renounce your right to judge them. Do this, and Jesus will set you free.

Chapter 3

A Stolen Adolescence

Entering my adolescent years, I began to lose faith and trust in my parents. My dad began to say things to me like "I know you'll soon be wanting to date, and since I'm your dad, I want you to let me show you what to expect when a boy tries to put his hands up your pants" (he was actually much more graphic, but I am choosing to leave out the details). I couldn't believe he was saying this. I was both shocked and offended. I wasn't even interested in dating, and what gave him the idea I would ever let anyone put their hands up my pants?

I worshipped the ground my dad walked on, but he was irresponsible. He always had difficulty holding down a job. He was a kid at heart and just never grew up. I went everywhere with him. Now I was finding excuses not to be around him, and especially not to be left at home alone with him.

One evening, my parents were engaged in a violent argument. Dad would just go crazy when he got angry at my mother. I stepped in between them and started to defend my mother. He picked up a scalding hot cup of coffee and threw it directly into my face. It was only a miracle of God that I didn't receive first- or second-degree burns on my face. My mother thought he was angry at me for defending her, but the truth was that he had tried unsuccessfully to have sex with me. He wanted me to believe that it was only because he loved me so much that he was willing to have sex with me. I may not have had a relationship with God at that time, but I knew this wasn't "love." I knew this was perverted, and I had no intention of giving in to him, whether I loved him or not.

My dad was working nights and sleeping during the day. My mother always had to work during the day. By the time summer came around and school was out, these attempts began to increase until they were weekly and sometimes daily, depending on who was around at the time. I started spending most of my time in my room, using every excuse I could think of to stay away from him.

One Saturday, my parents came home from shopping. Dad had decided, for no apparent reason, to buy a stereo for me, along with a few other smaller items. When he walked in with the stereo, I knew immediately what he was up to. We didn't have any money and certainly could not afford to spend it on unnecessary items. The following Monday, after my mother went to work, my dad approached me. He reasoned that he was being thoughtful by buying me this stereo in exchange for having sex with him. I refused and ran out of my room and out of the house. He went on a rampage; he ripped my telephone out of the wall and overturned my desk. He threw the stereo across my room as well as other objects within his reach. This was the worst I had ever seen him.

Even though I didn't have a relationship with God, I found myself praying constantly that He would protect me and not allow me to be in a situation that I couldn't get out of. But most of all, I prayed to God that He would protect my mother and brothers. I thought if I told my mother, she would either not believe me or, worse yet, make him leave. Then my brothers would no longer have a father. He was only approaching me, so I thought that I must be doing something to cause him to think I wanted to have sex with him. If I could figure out what I was doing, everything would be okay, and our family would remain intact.

In the ensuing summer months, I began wearing long-sleeve shirts with turtlenecks and long pants instead of shorts. This did not stop the advances. I couldn't find anything that would stop them, so I knew I must have some sinful problem that I wasn't aware of, and unless I could figure out what was causing this, my brothers risked losing their father.

To supplement our family's income, my dad started working on weekends, remodeling houses for real estate companies. He would go in and paint and clean their properties. I had no choice but to go and help him. At first, it wasn't too bad, but soon it became almost impossible to reject his advances. I would not go into the houses alone with him, and I would find any excuse possible not to go to work with him at all.

After a while, he became so busy (especially since I refused to work alongside him) that he needed extra help just to keep up with the workload. At that time, there was a young Native American man who lived in our neighborhood, and my dad started using him as part-time help. His name was Danuwoa (not his real name). I had never heard a name like this before. At first, I teased him about his name. It didn't seem to bother him, and he explained to me that it was a "generational" name that had been passed down from his family. His uncle was also given this name. I only met his uncle one time, but this uncle was Danuwoa's role model and was very proud of his Native American heritage.

Danuwoa lived on the reservation. He practiced and lived by Native American customs. He became consumed with me. He decided he wanted me to be his wife, and he would do whatever he had to do to "win" me, even though I was only fourteen.

As the pressure from my dad continued, I began to feel guilty for just existing. Danuwoa began to win my trust and became a means of escape from my dad. He also earned the trust of my parents, especially my mother.

Dad decided he would allow me to start dating Danuwoa. I assumed this was a ploy to somehow manipulate me so that I would eventually give in and have sex with him. Until now, I had not dated, but this could be the opening he was looking for—a possible change in my attitude toward boys and sex.

Danuwoa had a very masculine build. He was strong and had long auburn hair that went down his back, almost to his waist. He was an "Indian" and proud of it. He was known throughout the school as well as the neighborhood.

Even though I teased him about his name, no one else dared do so. He was violent. He had a rage about him, and you didn't want to be the one who caused him to become upset.

I remember six young men in our neighborhood who started harassing me. One of the guys wanted to date me, and he thought if he harassed me enough for dating "an Indian," I would agree to break off my relationship with Danuwoa. He started telling me that I would have "yellow" children if I eventually married Danuwoa. Finally, after the insults became vulgar, I had no choice but to tell Danuwoa. I was continually crying and upset over the things these guys were saying to me. Danuwoa confronted all six young men at one time. Four of them ran as fast as they could, but the other two were out of school for over a week due to bodily injuries. They never spoke to me again, but I still felt very guilty for them being hurt.

Even though Danuwoa became my protector and my excuse to get away from my dad, he became an even greater problem. He wanted total control of my every action. He was very jealous and possessive. I could not go anywhere or talk to anyone without him. Other students at school weren't even allowed to talk to me. We all knew who I could talk with and who I could not talk with. He started staying at my house every minute my dad would allow. The more possessive he became, the more I tried to get away from him. He knew this, but he wasn't going to let me go.

Danuwoa started spending a lot of time with my mother. He gave her the attention that my dad had never given her. In return, she would use her influence with me to try to keep me from ending the relationship with him. She would tell me how much he loved me and how deeply I was hurting him. She continued to lay guilt upon me even though I had little self-esteem left.

I remember looking around the living room. I would see Dad in his chair, thinking about how much I had loved and trusted him, but now I was so conflicted. I had to figure out ways to continue to keep a distance between us. I would see my mother and Danuwoa sitting on the sofa, laughing and talking. My brothers would be playing, and I would remember how I was totally responsible for the problems that were going on in my family. If my brothers were to continue to have a family, I would have to find a way to please everyone other than myself. I felt like I was being selfish if I did anything to please myself.

When I was fifteen and a half, I got a part-time job in a snack bar. Danuwoa was becoming more violent as well as more possessive. He would come to my place of work and sit and watch everyone I would talk to. I was not allowed to speak to anyone unless it was a customer, and only about their orders. He would watch, and if I disobeyed, he would get up, yell and scream, and cause a very embarrassing scene. This got so bad that the manager called me in and told me I would lose my job if Danuwoa didn't leave. He was not allowed on the premises, but he still wouldn't leave. After telling Dad, he made Danuwoa stay away from the snack bar, but he would still sit outside and send his friends in to check on me. I think my dad was the only person Danuwoa respected, but it was of no avail as I eventually lost my job because of him anyways.

I was in DECA (a national emerging business leaders club: Distributive Education Clubs of America) in high school and was required to hold a part-time job. I applied at a local variety store, and during the interview, Danuwoa came in and jerked me out of the interview. I was so embarrassed that I couldn't even face the lady in personnel. My DECA teacher had recommended me for this job, so when I told him what had happened, he called this lady and promised it would never happen again. By the grace of God, she gave me the job, but this didn't solve my problems with Danuwoa.

Danuwoa always picked me up after school to make sure I didn't see or speak with anyone that he didn't approve of. One particular afternoon, he wasn't there to pick me up. I thought it was strange, so I decided to walk home. We lived about two miles from the high school, and it took me about forty-five minutes to reach my house. When I entered the house, I couldn't find anyone, but Danuwoa's car was in the driveway. I stepped inside the doorway of my parents' bedroom and found Danuwoa and my mother in an intimate situation. I quietly stepped away; they never knew I was there. I knew that he had been giving my mother the love and attention that my dad wasn't giving her, and she had fallen in love with him. She had always been attracted to "Indian" men, and now this young, handsome man was giving her the attention she so needed and desired. Returning to the living room, Danuwoa realized I had walked home, and he apologized for not realizing how late it was. Though I was disturbed, I really wasn't totally upset because I reasoned that this may be an opportunity for me to get away from him.

The next day, I decided to tell him I no longer wanted to date him. In doing so, he threw me up against the wall, hitting my head on the edge of the telephone. He put his hands around my throat and started banging my head against the wall. He said I would never get away from him. My mother stepped in and tried to stop him, and all he said was "If you don't get away from me and stay out of this, I'll tell her and her dad everything!" My mom stepped back, and he eventually let go of me. Neither one of them was aware that I knew exactly what he meant. But I realized I would have to find another way to get away from him if I was going to protect my mother's secret.

Weeks passed, and he continued to get me in trouble at work. I finally told Dad that I didn't want to date him anymore. He said he would make sure he stayed away. This meant I would have to take a chance on Danuwoa telling my dad about the relationship between him and my mother, but I had reached the point where I had no other choice but to risk it. I continued to be tormented by guilt. Everything bad in my life and the lives of those I loved had happened because of me.

I began to block the feelings of guilt just to be able to function. After Danuwoa realized that I wasn't going to date him anymore, he became extremely violent, making serious threats on my life. They became so bad that I had to stay with family friends for several days. During that time, Danuwoa kicked in our front door and told Dad he was going to kill everyone if he didn't tell him where I was hiding. He left and began searching everywhere he knew to find me. Dad would take me to school, and the security guard would meet me either at the car or at the front entrance of the school. The guard would then escort me to each of my classes. Danuwoa was still a student at the school, and everyone knew how violent he was. One day during the exchange of classes, he passed me in the hall, stomped on my foot, and almost broke it. This resulted in him being removed from school property.

I had always made excellent grades, usually a 3.75–4.0 grade average. I had just started taking driver's education, and I was really excited about getting my driver's license. But when we would go out in the field to learn to drive, Danuwoa would be watching for the Driver's Ed car, and he would become very violent, making all sorts of threats. On the third day of class, he stopped the car and got into a physical altercation with the Driver's Ed instructor. The school administration decided that there was a real risk of injury not only to me but also to the other students. They decided to not allow me to continue in the Driver's Ed class. This was the first class I had ever failed, and my grade point average dropped significantly. Now, he was not only affecting my home life and my job, but he was also affecting my grades at school.

I had started working thirty to forty hours a week, and I was going to school full time. When I wasn't busy, I would just listen to my music and withdraw within myself, trying to figure out why bad things were always happening to me.

I have always had a heart for music. Music has always ministered to my soul and seemed to ease my pain, or so I thought. Unfortunately, the music I listened to during the early 70s ministered to my soul in a very destructive way. I remember the times I felt rejected and responsible for family problems. I would put my stereo headphones on and listen to Janis Joplin or Neil Young. Escaping into another world through the music, I would become very depressed, feeling unworthy of love or acceptance by anyone. This was a world where I could take all my hurts and pain, a place I would share with no one, not even God.

As I listened to this music and thought of the way I wished my life was, I would twist my hair around my fingers and pull as I rocked back and forth to the beat of the music. I did this while watching TV commercials for hair conditioners to prevent split ends. As I twisted my hair, I looked for split ends and pulled them out. What I did not understand at that time was that the stress of carrying the secrets of Mom's infidelity, Dad's sexual advances, and relational issues with Danuwoa, combined with the stress of balancing my workload and school, was too much for me to bear. The stress of life was causing me to literally pull my hair out. My pulling of split ends eventually became my coping mechanism for dealing with the stress. This was the beginning of a condition that was later diagnosed as trichotillomania (an anxiety-related compulsive disorder of pulling out hair). Perhaps I was angry at God and subconsciously removing the covering over me that was for my glory, as a reflection of His and a symbol of my submission to Jesus. Instead, I commiserated with Janis Joplin and Neal Young, who drew me deeper into depression.

Reflections of the Heart

I was the burden-bearer for my family's secrets. Between Mom's infidelity with my boyfriend and my dad pressuring me to have sex with him, the stress of those secrets created a destructive pattern in my attitude toward myself. What I did not recognize at that time was that my burden bearing stress was creating an anger in me that I was unable to resolve in a healthy manner. Music was my escape, and although it did ease my pain, it did not resolve nor bring healing to my root issues. My anger was building and being directed inwards, resulting in my hair pulling compulsive disorder (trichotillomania).

What I also did not recognize at that time was the influence of demonic attachments. There were spirits of shame, guilt, and unworthiness enslaving me to my emotional distress and disorder. These were lying spirits reminding me of how unworthy and unloved I was—that everything bad that happened to me was because I deserved it.

* * *

Do you carry secrets that have burdened you? They could be personal secrets or family secrets. Perhaps a friend, co-worker, or life partner has confided in you, but that secret has been a weight on your soul. Have shame and guilt been your companions? Do you blame yourself or God for your shame and guilt?

* * *

Professional counseling is good and advisable, but sometimes it's not enough. If you are also dealing with shame, self-hate, unworthiness, and even a death wish, especially if there is any tie to any kind of perversion, and counseling hasn't provided you with the peace you desire, then bring it to Jesus. If you believe there is a demonic stronghold binding you, then Jesus is your only solution.

Jesus is more than someone you can commiserate with. He is the Holy Counselor, and He is willing and able to supernaturally heal you of any emotional pain, hurt, or perversion. If you are feeling like any of this speaks to you, then I invite you to participate in the following prayer:

Through the eyes of your heart, picture Jesus as the Holy Counselor in front of you. Speak to Him, knowing with confidence that He neither judges you nor condemns you. Share your deepest secrets and burdens with Him. Once you've done that, it's time for you to listen. Listen to His gentle voice calling you to remember who you really are—a son or daughter of the King of the Highest Court. You are in Jesus, and He is in you, so let Him tell you what you mean to Him and how He feels about you. You are His beloved, and in Him you are safe. Now, in the presence of Jesus, command the demons that have tormented you over your secret burden to release you and send them to the feet of Jesus. Call them out by their associated negative characteristics: Command the spirits of shame, guilt, unworthiness, perversion, self-hate, death, and any others that come to mind to leave. They must obey under the authority of Jesus in you, especially in His presence. Finally, ask for His supernatural peace to come over you as you end your time with Him.

If after you've done this you still feel like you would like to talk to someone, find a trusted person, such as a pastor or Spirit-filled friend, who you can confide in as you openly confess your situation and secrets. Let him or her stand with you to present your requests to Jesus.

Chapter 4

Escape!

MY PARENTS USED TO GO OUT PARTYING AND DRINKING WITH their friends on Friday and Saturday nights. On one particular Saturday night, they had been partying until after 2:00 a.m. They were going to go out for breakfast with their friends, but they decided to come by the house on their way to the restaurant. My parents had met a young Native American man who was a family member of some of their friends. They thought this man, Jim, would be someone I might like to get acquainted with. My mother came and got me out of bed and introduced me to Jimmy Dale, and even though he was drunk, they felt it was safe for him to stay at the house with me while they went out for breakfast.

Dad thought Jim might be able to help me resist the temptation of allowing Danuwoa back into my life. By this time, Danuwoa had shifted from being physically violent to laying emotional guilt upon me, saying, "I can't live without you. If you don't come back to me, I'll kill myself."

Jim didn't seem to be a violent person, and my parents seemed to approve of him, so I began to spend time with him. He was four and a half years older than me (he was twenty). Jim didn't have a car or a job, and he lived in a house that didn't even have a bathroom, but he seemed like a nice guy. I didn't think there would be much risk in going out with him; at least it would get me out of the house and keep me busy.

Between school, my job, and Jim, there wasn't much time left for my dad to talk to me, much less try to make sexual advances. It seemed that just as quickly as the unwanted propositions had started, four years later, they stopped. Several times, I tried to talk with him about it, but he just acted like he didn't know what I was talking about. I never mentioned anything to my mother. I always knew that God had miraculously protected me from this terribly sinful act through my grandparents' prayers. I knew God's word said He would never allow you to experience more than you were capable of handling. God knew if my dad succeeded in molesting me, it would destroy my life completely. I praise God for His tender mercies being extended to me even when I rejected him.

When Danuwoa found out that I was dating Jim, he became extremely jealous. He would make threatening phone calls to me at home and at work. Things got so bad at work that the police had to remove him from the premises. Several times, he would sneak back in, and I would look up and see him watching every move I made. But then the police would come and remove him again. I think it would be safe to say I lived in constant fear!

One evening, he caught me in the front yard and said all he wanted to do was talk to me and he wouldn't hurt me. We went into the house, but Dad decided to make him leave. Danuwoa said he would hurt my dad if I didn't talk with him, so I convinced Dad to let him stay and talk. We sat on the sofa in front of my dad. Danuwoa whispered to me to go into the bedroom. He wanted to talk to me privately, but I refused. He finally pulled up the sleeve of his shirt to show me he had taken a knife and engraved my initial into his wrist. He had cut himself over and over, engraving the initial "J" into his skin. It would scab over, and then he would do it again. He did this until there was a thick scar in the shape of a "J" permanently engraved into his wrist. He reminded me that it would never go away, just as he would never go away. He said if I didn't go into the other room with him, he would take his knife to me. I refused to go with him, and he boldly picked me up off the sofa in front of my dad and started carrying me into the other room. I just started screaming because I knew he was going to really hurt me. My dad jumped up, and Danuwoa dropped me on the ground. Dad told him to get out and never come back, and he instructed me to call the police. He wasn't going to leave, but my mother was able to convince him to leave before the police arrived. Occasionally, he would listen to her. The next few months, he continued to harass me by telephone, but for the first time, I thought there might be a chance that I would get away from him.

I continued to see Jim. My mother would take me and drop me off at this place he was living at. I hesitate to call it a home since it didn't have any bathroom facilities or even running water for that matter, but it was somewhere to go. Jim was a musician. He was always writing and singing songs. He loved to listen to Bob Dylan, Leon Russell, and a lot of folk music. One night, I went to his place, but he wouldn't answer the door. I could hear music in the background. My mother had left me there, and it was very cold outside. I had no choice but to go in. I found Jim passed out on the floor. At first, I thought he was drunk, but he had this terrible smell about him. For the first time in my life, I came face to face with a person who got high sniffing glue and paint. He had paint and glue all around his mouth and nose. I couldn't believe anyone did this. After he came to, he promised he would never do it again. I was naïve enough to believe him.

I continued to see Jim, but not long after that, I started feeling sorry for Danuwoa. I knew he thought he really loved me, and I felt so guilty for him loving me so much. Guilt drove me, and I started dating both Danuwoa and Jim.

The summer I turned sixteen was a very difficult year for me and my mother. We argued about everything. I felt like I couldn't do anything right. Danuwoa was constantly at our house again, and I knew I had to get away from him. When I dated Jim, Mom would disapprove, encouraging me to date Danuwoa. One evening, I felt like I was going to explode. I got into a terrible argument with her. I remember running out the back door of our house. I ran all the way to the back fence but couldn't go any further. I sat down with my head between my legs and my hands on top of my head. My mother caught me and slapped my face, hitting me repeatedly.

I knew God's word said I had to respect and honor my parents, but I knew I had to get away. I fought my way past Mom, and I walked as far as I could, but then Danuwoa came and found me. He took me home, and I had to face the wrath of my dad even though I didn't feel I had done anything wrong. I tried to keep my composure, and my outward behavior was nothing like the eruption I was feeling on the inside. I felt like I was going insane. I spent all my energy just trying to keep an outward appearance of stability. In spite of all I was feeling, I was still trying to convince myself that I had a loving family.

I was living a lie, thinking that there were many who would have loved to be in my place, living the life I had with loving parents. The issues I had had to be my fault. All I had to do was figure out what my problem was and solve it. This was one of the worst arguments I had ever had with my mother.

A few days later, my throat closed, and I could not swallow. My mom and Danuwoa took me to the emergency room because I was having a difficult time breathing. At this time, I had no understanding of what or why this was happening to me.

I could have gone to live with my grandparents, but by this time, I was bringing in additional income for my family, and they wouldn't have been able to survive without it. My brothers needed me, and I promised I would never leave them again. Beyond that, I recognized that my liberal lifestyle would not be tolerated by my structured and strict grandparents. Submitting to their lifestyle would be like living in prison. There were rules upon rules: I could read the *Reader's Digest* but not the newspaper; I couldn't go swimming if boys were there; I couldn't go to movie theaters, I couldn't wear any makeup, not even clear nail polish. I couldn't imagine living the way they did. Besides that, they probably wouldn't understand me.

We had gone to spend Easter with my grandparents that year. I was so excited about seeing them. I was working and had bought a new, fashionable dress to wear for Easter. When we got to the parsonage, I ran around to the back of the church to hug my grandfather. When he saw me, he said, "Get in the house, and get that dress off. I'm so ashamed of you. You're not welcome in my home dressed like that!" This devastated me. I hadn't brought a change of clothes, and I had to spend the rest of the day with him staring at me with his disapproval. My grandfather, the only one who I thought loved me unconditionally, was putting a condition on his love. I knew I would never be able to measure up to his expectations again. I had let him down.

I soon began to feel that God's love was conditional, just as my grandfather's love had become conditional. I convinced myself that God would only accept me if I were perfect. I knew I had caused the people I loved a great deal of pain, so God would never love me unless I was able to earn it. But I wasn't going to waste my time trying to convince God that I deserved His love; I knew I didn't deserve it. I was too selfish and bad for Him to love me.

It didn't take much thought for me to realize that if I was going to get away from my parents, the only way I could do it would be to get married. My parents' friends all had daughters, and they were all getting married that summer. I knew my dad would not allow me to marry Danuwoa, and he was too young to marry without his parents' signature. In addition to that, I didn't want to marry him because that would give him a legal right, in his eyes, to really abuse me physically, and I knew he would kill me if I ever tried to get away from him. My next and only other choice was Jim. Even though he drank quite a bit and did glue and paint once in a while, I could have done and deserved worse! I thought that if we got married, I could change him.

On December 9, 1972, Jim and I were married. Danuwoa hot-rodded his car up and down the streets in front of the church, and I feared that at any time he would come charging into the church and kill everyone. As Dad walked me down the aisle, I began to cry uncontrollably. Dad had told me I didn't have to get married if I really didn't want to, even though he had spent money he really didn't have to make sure I had a nice wedding. He said he would forgive me even if "I selfishly threw away his hard-earned money." I was guilt-ridden. Still, I almost backed out, but I couldn't overcome my guilty feelings. So, the wedding proceeded, and vows were exchanged.

Jim and I lived in an old, dumpy duplex in a rather bad part of town, and at night Danuwoa would race his car back and forth in front of the house, keeping me in a continuous state of fear. I became increasingly aware of Jim having not only an alcohol problem but also a serious drug problem. He couldn't hold down a job, so he began selling drugs on the side.

Since he was a musician, he would go to jams on the weekends. One Saturday night, he insisted that I go with him. I did not know Jim to be a violent person, but now that we were married, I was beginning to experience some verbal as well as physical abuse. I was still going to school, and now I was holding down a full-time job, so I was exhausted and didn't want to go. I tried to get him to let me stay home, but he wouldn't let me. Finally, at 4:30 a.m., I decided I was leaving with or without him. He still didn't have a job at this time, but I had to be at work the next day. I had to get some rest. He refused to leave, so without him knowing it, I took the car and went home. About 8:30 a.m., I woke up to Jim having his hands around my neck, telling me he was going to kill me. No one would ever embarrass him the way I had embarrassed him by leaving him without transportation. One of his friends had to inconveniently drive him home. He physically beat me and raped me to make sure I understood that I would live to regret it if I ever embarrassed him again.

This was all I needed to leave. I told him if he ever laid a hand on me again, I would leave. I had suffered enough physical abuse from men. Now I had a job and could support myself. I certainly didn't need him. Strangely enough, I thought Jim's violence was related to something I had done to him. He hadn't been violent until we married, so I reasoned that this must also be my fault. I was determined to get away from him. But I was also fleeing from the additional guilt I was feeling because of his violence. I started looking for reasons and even instigated some arguments to try to get him to hit me so I could honor my threat and leave.

Beyond his violence and my guilt, his drug problem became increasingly worse. I began to look at him with disgust. I never loved this guy; I never even liked him. I only married him to get away from my parents. I used him just like people had used me all my life, so I realized I had to find a way to leave even if I could not provoke him to violence. But as his drug addiction deepened, he became more jealous and violent. He also began to drink very heavily, taking all of the money I made just to support his drinking and drug habits. I couldn't work enough hours to make enough money to satisfy him, and so the second semester of my senior year of high school, I dropped out.

I couldn't continue with school, Jim's demands, and a full-time job. I knew if I stayed in school, I would have to cut back my hours at work, but I wouldn't have enough money to leave him (to pay for the divorce). So, I realized that there was only one person who loved me enough and was strong enough to get me out of my situation—Danuwoa! I called him and told him I was in danger, that I wanted to leave Jim and needed his help getting away. Just as I knew he would, he told me he would help me get out safely.

When I would go to the laundry mat or the grocery store, I would call Danuwoa and tell him where to meet me. We would secretly meet and plan how I would get out. I shared a bond with Danuwoa that is difficult to explain. I knew I could count on him. In a strange way, I felt he was honorable. The entire time we were together, I never had sex with Danuwoa. He said he loved me, and he would never pressure me into having sex until I had married him, and Danuwoa always honored his word. That was one reason I was so fearful of him. He also honored his threats!

Jim told me he was working. He would get up and leave each morning. He was working drug deals, but the money was being used to buy his own drug supply. One afternoon, he met with a drug friend who told him that he had seen me with Danuwoa. He came home, stormed into the house, and started physically abusing me, telling me he was aware that I had been meeting with Danuwoa. I had embarrassed him in front of his friends, even after he had warned me to never embarrass him again. After he hit me several times in the face, I told him I was leaving, and I walked out the door.

I walked seven miles to my parent's home. When I walked in, my dad asked what I was doing there. I told him I had left Jim and I was moving back home. He asked what had happened to my face, and I told him I had been hit in the face with a door at work. I was repeating the pattern of protecting someone who shouldn't have been protected. I believed that everything was my fault, and now this marriage was ending in divorce just because of my selfishness.

Danuwoa was excited to see that I had left and began to make his presence available at all times, using the excuse that he was there to protect me. He felt I must really love him, or I wouldn't have called him for help. But love had nothing to do with it. I needed physical protection, and I had come to realize that love wasn't real, at least not for a person like me. I was miserable, and I deserved every bad thing that had happened in my life. I just needed to learn how to live with it.

Jim started calling, begging me to come back. One night, he called and said there had been a contract placed on his life by some drug dealers. They wanted him dead. He gave the usual line about how he couldn't live without me, begging me to come back. I refused and hung up the phone. After about an hour, I really became uncomfortable. I thought something was terribly wrong, so I called the police and asked them to check on him. I decided to go to the duplex to check for myself. As I reached the duplex, there was an ambulance out front. Apparently, Jim was so stoned on drugs, alcohol, paint, and glue that when he bent down to light the bathroom heater, he passed out from the gas fumes. It was a miracle that he didn't burn the place down. He had laid there passed out for over an hour with gas fumes escaping from the heater. They hauled him off to the hospital. As I saw him, I realized he hadn't had a bath in more than three or four weeks. He smelled of alcohol, drugs, paint, glue, and filth. I couldn't believe I had ever married this man, no matter how desperate I thought I was. Medics took him to the hospital, so I didn't have to be concerned anymore. I returned home to my parents.

In February, I had been married for two months, and that was long enough for me! I was ready for a divorce, but I didn't have any money to obtain counsel. After several months, Jim moved into a "fruit stand" on the outskirts of our city. He called and asked if he could see me. I agreed, but my parents were furious and forbade me to see him. I went anyway. As he talked, he said he was off drugs and that he was working for the owners of this fruit stand. He was trying to get his life back together. Would I agree to come back on a trial basis? I didn't want to, but I told him I would consider it.

Meanwhile, Danuwoa had again become very possessive. I was suffocating just being in the room with him. When I returned home, Danuwoa had found out I had met with Jim, and he had told my parents. They were all very angry with me. My dad took my car keys away from me and forbade me to go anywhere. That was just how crazy my life had become. I was seventeen years old, married but separated, and working on a divorce. I was holding down a full-time job, not only to support myself but also to help support my parents and brothers. I was making car payments, and now I was grounded! My car was the only means I had of escaping when things got difficult. I could always drive around and think things through, but now I couldn't even do that. It was my sanctuary, the only place I felt safe. Now I felt trapped, and it made me furious.

My parents went out of town that weekend, and they left me in the care of Danuwoa. They were concerned I would leave and go back to Jim while they were gone. I had planned to do just that; after all, my dad was so unfair in his punishment. Danuwoa was told by my parents not to stay at the house with me but to watch what I was up to. Danuwoa was clever. That Saturday evening, the telephone rang. I answered it. It was Danuwoa, and he said, "I just wanted to check and see if you were okay." I replied, "I'm okay." Then, very quickly, he said, "I have to go now. I just wanted to check on you. Bye." Then he hung up the phone. I thought it was a very strange conversation, but I just disregarded it. After a while, I called out to the "fruit stand" to talk with Jim. He answered the telephone, but he couldn't hear anything I was saying. I hung up and went next door to ask our neighbors if I could use their phone. My neighbor decided that if I had already received a call on our phone, he would come over and see what the problem was. Upon examining our two telephones, he realized that someone had removed the mouthpieces inside the receivers. I could hear the person calling, but no one could hear me. Danuwoa had cleverly managed to sneak into our house while I was napping and removed the mouthpieces. He then called me, making his conversation very quick, and asked only one question, knowing I would probably just answer "okay" to his question (and that's exactly what I did). I was so furious. I made up my mind; I was leaving and going back to Jim. I returned with my neighbor to his house and called a taxi to come and get me.

I moved into this fruit stand with Jim. It was one open room with only three side walls. Everything was open to the outside. There was no plumbing of any kind. No restroom facilities. A small area about the size of a closet was located off the back part of the room. There was a roach infested mattress on the floor to sleep on and more flies than you can count. There were no sheets, blankets, pillows—nothing but this dirty mattress. There was a service station across the street, so I did have a place to go to use the restroom. My parents still had my car. I had no transportation. Jim managed to get different friends of his to provide my means of transportation back and forth to work. I have always had a very keen sense of smell, and the smell of rotten fruit made me feel nauseous. I have always been a very clean person, so I found myself walking ten miles on most days to my girlfriend's house just to be able to take a bath. Thankfully, she would give me a ride back to where I needed to go.

The man who owned the fruit stand dealt heavily in drugs and drug smuggling. He would make monthly trips to Mexico and bring back merchandise from Mexico to sell in this fruit stand. He would use this as a cover to smuggle in drugs. The fruit stand was located on a corner where two counties met. The building itself was in Cleveland County. However, if you stepped across the street, you were in Oklahoma County. In the early 70s, you could only be arrested for dealing drugs by narcotics agents who worked in the county the drugs were sold in. So, if narcotics agents from Cleveland County came after you, all you had to do was step across the street into Oklahoma County. If Oklahoma County narcotics agents came after you, you stepped across the street into Cleveland County. The only way they could ever arrest you would be if both Cleveland and Oklahoma County agents were there at the same time. Everyone knew this would never happen. In addition, there were police officers from both counties who were buying drugs at this fruit stand. So, the owner of the fruit stand would bring in the drugs, Jim would sell them, and he would receive free drugs for being the middleman with very little risk of being arrested. I was supposed to be stupid and not realize what they were doing. I may have made some bad decisions, but I'm not stupid. I knew exactly what they were doing.

One Saturday night, Jim had been making some pretty good deals. He also had a good supply of cocaine for his own use. He had been drinking and started loading up. His attitude became very violent, and I knew I had better stay out of his way. After I realized how out of control he was, I decided I would go back to the back room. As much as I hated the thought of doing it, I decided I would lay down on the mattress, go to sleep, and stay out of his way. Until this time, I always slept in a chair because I couldn't stand the filth. I finally managed to fall asleep. I had been asleep for about an hour, and I woke up with something on my chest and a sharp blade at my throat. Jim was sitting on top of my chest. He used both of his knees to keep my arms pinned down. This sharp blade was a machete he had brought back from Mexico. The blade reached from my left ear to my right ear. It was cold and sharp. When I tried to say something, Jim told me to shut up, and he would press the knife harder against my throat. I will never forget that feeling! Jim was out of his mind in a drug induced craze. He said I was a dog. The same dog that had been sent to murder his dad. He said I was just an evil presence sent to kill him because he (Jim) was the only one who had information about his dad's murder. He said he was going to kill me just like I had killed his dad. Jim's dad, Jessie, had been murdered several years earlier, and they never found out who murdered him or why he had been murdered. Someone entered his home, killed him while he was passed out drunk on the sofa, and then set his house on fire with Jesse still in it. I was past fear. This was my end!

This went on for about twenty minutes. I finally closed my eyes and prayed, "God, I don't want to die, but it looks like this is it. Please watch over my brothers, but if you save me this time, I will return home and do whatever my parents ask me to do. I will give my life to you and never ask for anything again. If you'll just help me this one last time, I promise I won't be selfish ever again."

Immediately, Jim passed out completely. I pushed him off of me, and at 3:00 a.m. in the morning, I started walking the eight miles it took to get to my parent's house. Since I was outside the city limits, there were several cars with drunks and abusive men who stopped and tried to get me into their cars, but just as He always has, Father God protected me all the way to my parent's home.

Reflections of the Heart

In my teens, I never felt that I was worthy of anything good. My identity and self-worth were tied to and limited by my life experiences. I was enslaved by a poverty mindset.

Love was only experienced as expressed through my dysfunctional parents. I never understood God's unconditional love and acceptance. Even my grandparents, who loved the Lord and whom I cherished deeply, had conditions upon which I could receive their love and acceptance.

Life choices for me were not based on love but on how to escape a living hell, and often this felt like I had no choice. I escaped my dad's furtive sexual advances through my relationship with Danuwoa. I escaped Danuwoa's jealousy, violence, and overbearing possessiveness as well as my parents' manipulative and dysfunctional relationship by marrying Jim. I escaped Jim by using Danuwoa (again).

I know now that I did have choices, but I simply did not recognize my options. Doing things my way did not result in freedom, but rather led me into a deeper pit. I was abused and bruised; I was emotionally distraught, and I wished I were dead. At any time, I could have called upon Jesus for His wisdom and submitted myself to Him for His guidance. Looking back, I know the decisions I made seem like pure foolishness, but know this: at that point in my life, all I knew was based upon my collective life experiences. I really felt that I was trapped and that my only choice was to escape using any means available to me.

* * *

Reflect back on your life. Are there decisions you've made that you wish you could take back? Or perhaps you are in the midst of a difficult choice right now. How will you make a potentially life-changing decision? Do you pray or talk to God before you make critical decisions? Do you think God is controlling and manipulative or kind and loving? How does your understanding of God influence how you make critical decisions?

*   *   *

I want to assure you that God can and will redeem you no matter how poorly you chose. He will not change the events or the circumstances surrounding your choices. But Jesus will bring you into healing and wholeness, regardless of the consequences of your choices. No matter how badly your soul has been damaged, He will restore you.

If you feel trapped and are in a difficult situation, I invite you to set the eyes of your heart upon Jesus. It's okay to look upon Him even if it feels like you're using your imagination to do so. Your imagination is God's gift to you so that you can see Him. Do not think about tomorrow or the next day and the troubles it brings. Look upon Jesus and say to Him, "Jesus, at this very moment, I give to you my whole heart, mind, and will. I submit my whole self to you and ask you for your supernatural peace and your supernatural wisdom to help me make wise choices, if only for this very moment. Help me with courage and give me hope that is based upon your faithfulness and not my abilities or my unbelief. Let me experience the presence of your Holy Spirit dwelling with me to give me the strength I need for today. Amen."

If you have made a bad choice and are currently feeling trapped and/ or living in an abusive situation or are in crisis at this moment, get yourself out of the situation. If you are living in the United States, there is help available to you and crisis hot lines operating throughout the nation. Search the internet for contact information (or try the National Domestic Violence Hotline at 800-799-7233). If you are distraught, depressed, or have suicidal thoughts, please contact the National Suicide Prevention Lifeline (800-273-8255) or search the internet for other help resources.

Chapter 5

A New but Tragic Start

IT WAS NOW THE END OF APRIL 1973. I WENT TO CHURCH THE NEXT Sunday evening, and at age seventeen, I rededicated my life to God in a local Assembly of God Church. I went directly home and called my grandparents to let them know. Unfortunately, from their perspective, I wasn't in the correct denomination. I accepted Christ as a child in my grandparents' church, and to be saved, I had to be in their denomination. But I just couldn't really live according to their doctrines. I knew God wanted me to be at the church where I rededicated myself to Him.

Now, I was a born-again Christian (again, if childhood counts), but I still had a problem to deal with—Danuwoa. By this time, he was beginning to pressure me to have sex with him, which I never intended to do. I continued to resist. I tried to keep myself as busy as possible with work so I wouldn't have to deal with him anymore. I had decided for sure that I would divorce Jim. If I didn't, I would probably end up dead at his hands.

Gail, a girlfriend I worked with, invited me to go out with her and her boyfriend one weekend. There was a downtown hangout called "Hollie's." My dad had repeatedly forbidden me to go there. It was just a drive-in that served hamburgers, soft drinks, and beer, but it had a reputation for having a rough crowd of people hanging around. My dad was worried about me hanging out with a rough crowd of people. It's funny and ironic given that he was the one who brought Jim home from a bar to meet me.

All my friends did drugs, but by God's grace, I never once did drugs, drank alcohol, or smoked a cigarette. I didn't even drink coffee. I was entertained watching everyone else make fools of themselves. Even though my self-worth had been lost several years earlier, I didn't feel compelled to join in on their folly to be accepted. I was a contrarian and always went against the flow of the popular crowd. So now I was ready for a "rough group of people." I needed a change of friends. If my friends seemed nice to my parents, maybe it was time for a change.

Gail's boyfriend was a member of the Oklahoma City Corvette Club. He drove a new Corvette, and he had a friend he wanted me to meet. They always met at Hollie's on Friday and Saturday nights. I went with them to meet his friend Charles.

Charles was different than anyone I had ever met. He drove a new pearl white Corvette, and he had painted red stripes and blue stars on it. It was fabulous! He was very polite and courteous. He even bought me something to eat and drink, and I didn't have to pay for it! That was a first for me. The only problem I had with him was that he was a military brat with a regulation-style haircut. He wore nice dress clothes, but even worse, he wore shoes! I had never dated anyone who had short hair or didn't wear bell-bottom blue jeans. How would I ever get him out of his shoes, much less suggest that he grow his hair out, at least past his shoulders? This may sound strange, but remember I grew up during the height of the "hippie culture" of the 60s and early 70s, and while I did not get into "free love and drugs," my tastes in fashion were most definitely affected by it. But now that I was a born-again Christian, I decided I would try to overlook these faults of his!

Looking back, it's hard for me to believe what I was thinking at that time. We drove around town in his car, talking about everything. No man had ever talked to me, much less asked me to express my opinion about something, so this was quite unusual. At about midnight, he took me back to my car, which I had parked across the street from Hollie's. He gave me his phone number and said he was going to the lake the next day. He asked me to call and let him know if I wanted to go with him. I really wanted to, but he didn't really know anything about me. He didn't know I was in the process of getting a divorce, and I certainly wasn't going to tell him about this violent curse called Danuwoa that followed me everywhere I went.

As we approached my car, I saw Danuwoa sitting on the hood, just waiting for me. One of his friends had seen me leave with Charles. He called Danuwoa, who had decided to teach me a lesson. I wasn't allowed to date anyone except him, ever again. Charles didn't know what was going on. He didn't know who Danuwoa was or why he was sitting on my car. As I got out of Charles' Corvette, Danuwoa started screaming and running toward me in what sounded like a Native American war cry! Charles was pulling away from the curb, but he stopped to see if I needed him to stay. I assured him I knew this guy and that I was capable of controlling the situation. I asked him to please leave and not come back to check on me. Hesitantly, Charles finally left. What I was really afraid of was that Danuwoa was going to jump on top of his Corvette and do some serious damage to it. Then this poor caring guy, who did nothing but be nice to me, would get the daylights beat out of him.

Danuwoa had ripped some wires out from under the hood of my car, so I couldn't leave. He pushed me up against his car and had about four or five of his friends come watch what he was going to do to me. He had a revolver with a silencer on it. For about thirty minutes, he put this gun next to my temple and asked his friends what he should do. Should he shoot me or not?

His friends kept telling him that I deserved to be shot. After all, I had humiliated him. First, I was his girlfriend, and then I married Jim. He was good enough to take me back, even after I had sex (with my husband). Now I was seen in front of his friends with Charles.

About this time, a police officer came by patrolling the area. I tried to get his attention, but Danuwoa and his friends blocked his view, so he couldn't see what was going on. I knew Danuwoa was true to his threats, so I was terrified. But I didn't want him to know how fearful I really was.

Danuwoa put me in the front seat on the passenger's side of his car. He got in next to me with his beer and his gun. He opened the chamber of the gun and showed me that there were two bullets in the chamber. He put the gun next to my head for a second time, and for nearly three and a half hours, he drank his beer, spun the revolver, and pulled the trigger. I was expecting a bullet each time. He reminded me that he couldn't live without me, so he decided just to kill me instead.

There was a song that was very popular in '73 called "Without You." The first few lines of the song were "I can't live if living is without you, I can't live, I can't live anymore!" (Harry Nilsson, "Without You," released in 1971). Danuwoa played this song over and over, spinning the chamber and pulling the trigger repeatedly. He said if I lived through the night, it was only due to fate. Did God provide a miracle here? What are the chances of a gun being triggered again and again for almost four hours and not firing?

Finally, the sun was coming up. Danuwoa was getting tired and maybe a bit more sober. I don't know if he believed that fate was on my side or if daylight changed his mood, but he was willing to listen to me. Though I was tired and numbed from hours of trauma, I found my voice. I convinced him that my dad would be out looking for me. I was able to negotiate with him. I told him I wouldn't see Charles anymore and I wouldn't tell my dad what he had done this evening. My dad was the only person who Danuwoa respected. I told Danuwoa that if he wanted to stay in my dad's good graces, he had better get me home. He reluctantly agreed and took me home.

Dad was up waiting for me, and I had to face his wrath. He wasn't interested in what had happened. He only wanted to know where my car was. I told him it had broken down and was parked across the street from Hollie's. Then he was really upset since he had forbidden me to ever go to Hollie's. The next morning, my dad told Danuwoa he had better go get my car and bring it home, which he did gladly.

My parents were going to be out of town all day, so I decided to call Charles and take him up on his offer to go to the lake. I gave him instructions on how to get to my house. Unfortunately, I didn't give very good instructions. He missed our street and ended up going right past Danuwoa's house. Now Charles was the only one in Oklahoma City with a red, white, and blue Corvette, and Danuwoa knew exactly who he was. As soon as I saw Charles pull up in the driveway, I ran out and got in the car.

Evidently, Danuwoa had entered our house through the back door, and as Charles and I drove off, Danuwoa ran out the front door in a violent rage. As we drove away, I watched Danuwoa pounding and kicking my car with his hands and feet. I didn't want to tell Charles about what was going on. I thought if I told him, I would scare him off. I knew it would happen sooner or later, but I was hoping it would be later.

Charles knew I was afraid to go home before my parents returned, so he decided to take me to meet his mother. I'll never forget her first words. Charles introduced me to her, and she asked him, "What bar did you pick this b**** up in?" I knew she was going to be a delight to know! I went home when my parents returned.

Charles had asked if I wanted to go out again the next night. We agreed that he would pick me up at 7:00 p.m. Monday night, he called and canceled, saying he had to work late. I presumed that Charles had an encounter with Danuwoa. I thought I would never see him again.

Every time I wanted to date anyone other than Danuwoa, he would wait down the street, and when he saw some guy approaching my house, he would stop them and bash their face in. Besides that, if Danuwoa didn't get to Charles, his mother would. I knew she disapproved of me. She thought I wasn't good enough for her son. I really understood how she felt because I felt the same way.

To my surprise, on Tuesday, Charles called and asked me to go to dinner. No one had ever taken me out to a restaurant. He took me for my first pizza, and he didn't even ask me to pay for it! As we talked that night, I told him about Danuwoa and that I thought he had approached Charles. Charles quickly replied, "Oh, he already approached me. We had a confrontation Sunday night after I left your house. He tried to get violent with me, but I just explained to him how it was really going to be. I was not leaving, and if he had a problem with that, we could just deal with it now!" Charles never told me what happened after that. All I knew and still know today is that Danuwoa never bothered me again. I couldn't believe it. Just one confrontation, and Charles took care of my continuing "curse of Danuwoa."

Charles and I started dating every night. After about three weeks, I had missed my menstrual cycle for a second month. It had only been ten weeks since I had left Jim, and I thought for sure I was pregnant. I went to Charles and told him I couldn't date him any longer. I explained that I thought I was pregnant and that it would be an interracial baby. Charles came from a very strict Irish Catholic family. His mom already hated me, and I knew what she would say once this came out. But what came next surprised me. I never expected the reply I received from Charles. He asked me if I was going to continue with the divorce. I said yes. He said, "If you're not married, what does a baby have to do with my love for you? A baby is a baby, deserving of love no matter what the circumstances are behind his or her conception." This guy was beyond anything I could have ever imagined. For the first time in many years, I had received unconditional love, and from a "Catholic" of all things. Two days later, I started my cycle. Praise God, I wasn't pregnant, but it took the thought of that possibility for me to realize what kind of sincere, loving person Charles was. I decided it wasn't important that he didn't have long hair and that I could deal with him wearing shoes, but I definitely had to do something about the knit dress slacks. I finally convinced him to buy two pairs of blue jeans. We went over to see his mother, but she refused to let him in the door with jeans on, and of course, I could never come in unless I had on shoes and a bra!

The fact that Charles was Catholic presented a new problem. My dad was not a religious man. He knew nothing about Christianity. I remember when I was young, my parents and I visited a little church in our neighborhood. Dad sat on the back pew. When the services concluded, the pastor came over and shook my dad's hand. He said, "Sir, are you a Christian?" Dad replied, "Oh, no! I'm not a Christian, I'm a Baptist!" I don't say this as an insult to Baptists. I only use it to illustrate how ignorant my dad was when it came to Christianity. He had an aunt who went to a Baptist church. Since she was a "Baptist," he thought he must be one too.

His bias against Catholics was even greater than his black bias. He would always tell me, "Never bring a Catholic into my house. I would rather see you date and marry a black man before I'd ever allow you to date or marry a Catholic." I never told my dad Charles was a committed Catholic.

By the time we were married, Dad had begun to like Charles. Charles spoiled my dad just like he did me, so it didn't matter if he was a Catholic! Praise God, our Father is so merciful to us, His children, even when we don't deserve mercy.

The Danuwoa problem was solved, but now I was having "Jim problems" again. He would call and tell me he was going to kill himself. Finally, I had decided no one would keep me from dating Charles. I had never met anyone like him before, and no guilt would cause me to lose him. Jim called one Saturday night. He was drunk and high on drugs! He said he had a gun and was going to kill himself. I told him to go ahead and do it. I didn't care, and I never wanted him to call me again. If he couldn't do it, he should just let me know, and I would gladly come over and do it for him. I knew he was a coward, and he would never be able to pull the trigger, or so I thought. But he did shoot himself; only he was so drunk that he shot himself in the foot. That night, God miraculously removed him from my life, and I have not seen or heard from or about him since.

On my eighteenth birthday, my lawyer and I stood before a judge in Oklahoma County and petitioned for my divorce. My dad had given me enough money to retain counsel, and Charles gave me the last $200 I needed to get the divorce. Here I stood, eighteen years old, and I had already lived a life full of fear, more than most people experience in an entire lifetime.

Charles and I dated every night until we were married, except for the Monday nights he had to work late. In fact, after eight weeks, Charles moved in with me and my parents.

My uncle was a minister in Arizona. He came for a visit in July. He was always concerned about me, and when he met Charles, he encouraged me to marry this guy as soon as possible. I guess he just thought someone would scare him away, and he knew Charles was good for me. I explained to him that I had to wait six months before I could remarry in the state of Oklahoma. He advised me that in Arizona, there was only a forty-eight-hour waiting period and that we didn't have to be Arizona residents. So, in October of 1973, we headed out for Arizona to be married by my uncle. Charles sold his Corvette just to get enough money to buy a more economical car and cover the expense of our trip to Arizona. Now, I really knew he loved me.

After we married, Charles gave me the world! He convinced me that I could do anything I desired to do. He immediately demanded that I go back and finish school. He taught me to set goals for myself and work as hard as I could to achieve them. If there was something I couldn't do, it was only because I didn't want it badly enough. His high self-esteem is one thing that I always admired about him, and now, for the first time in my life, I was beginning to rebuild my self-esteem, or so I thought.

We got caught up in materialism, and by the time we had been married two months, we had more material possessions than my parents had collected in over twenty-two years of marriage. Our material possessions were nice and expensive. Charles had been blessed by God with the ability to make money, so we lived a very comfortable lifestyle. I guess you could say he spoiled me rotten! He became the answer to all of my problems.

We purchased our first home only eleven blocks from my parents'. I thought that since I was married, their demands on me would become less. Jeff, my youngest brother, was upset because I wouldn't let him live with us. He thought I should allow him to live with us because I had promised I would never leave him. He would get up around 7 a.m., walk over to our house, and ring the doorbell until I would let him in. One morning, I lost my temper with him and told him he could not come back unless I came over and picked him up. He left crying and said I didn't love him anymore.

A few days later, Mom called me in the morning in a hysterical state. She said something was wrong with Jeff. I immediately got dressed and went to their house. I found Jeff in violent convulsions, swallowing his tongue. I remember picking him up in my arms, and as I was heading for the car, my mom just stood there screaming. Mom has always been very dramatic with her emotions, but this day, I didn't have time to put up with her. I informed her that I was taking Jeff to the hospital with or without her. We all got into the car, and I took Jeff to the nearest emergency room. From there, he was transferred to Children's Hospital, and we knew something was very seriously wrong.

Jeff spent weeks in the hospital. They finally concluded that he had a rare and incurable disease, and he only had a few more months left. I sat with him. I slept with him. My mother felt she couldn't miss her work because they needed the money, so I stayed with Jeff every moment I could. I felt so guilty because I promised I would always take care of him. One night I told him, "Jeff, we just bought a new two-story house. I know how you have always wanted to live in a two-story house and have your own room, so I promise that when you get better, I'll let you come and live with me. I'll never leave you again." Jeff was only ten. He always had this mischievous smile on his face. Jeff looked at me and said, "Sissy, I can't come and live with you. Didn't you see the two angels that came to see me this morning? They said that Jesus had sent them to see me and tell me not to be afraid. He wants me to come and live with Him, and they are going to come back and get me in just a few days. I really want to go with them to be with Jesus if that's okay with you."

A few weeks before Jeff got sick, he had spent some time with my grandparents. He had accepted Jesus as his savior and had been baptized by my grandfather. Now this little boy was telling me not to worry about him anymore because Jesus was taking care of him now. The next day, Jeff slipped into a coma and never regained consciousness. He was moved to a convalescent home and died only two days after his tenth birthday, on September 13, 1974.

I'll never forget the guilt I felt. If I had not been selfish and let him live with me, he surely wouldn't have died. I was also angry, and I blamed my parents for his death. If they had been good parents, Jeff would not have become ill. I was tormented by the memory of my pregnant mother saying over and over that she wished he were dead.

Now, my mother was using his death to milk every emotional opportunity she could get, just to get attention. I was angry and frustrated because she was making this situation all about her instead of being all about Jeff's short and tragic life! I found it very difficult to even be around my parents after this. I was angry and consumed with guilt. I just wanted them to leave me alone, but I was ashamed of these feelings and could never tell anyone, so I just continued being the responsible daughter I had always been.

Jene was left to be the only child at home. He used every opportunity he could to bring guilt upon my parents. He went from being the middle, neglected son to the only child at home. Because my parents felt guilt over Jeff, they soon began to overcompensate with Jene. So he learned how to manipulate them to get his way.

Reflections of the Heart

Though I had accepted Jesus in my childhood, it was during this period of my life that I had a born-again Christian experience, which started me on a new path. I am so grateful for the path He has directed me to. I rejected my old ways and found new doors opening for me, which I gladly stepped through. I have experienced much grace, deep healing, and freedom in my life starting from this point, but my life was not and still is not a "fairy tale." I did not have a "happily ever after" turning point even after I accepted Jesus or after I married Charles. Trauma and tragedy still plagued me.

I suffered from a form of post-traumatic stress disorder (PTSD) even before it became well understood. I hesitate to put that in writing because in no way do I want to downplay the severe trauma experienced by our vets in Vietnam and Afghanistan. I also don't want to compare my experiences to theirs. I do not relive the traumatic events of my life that paralyze me from functioning. At the same time, I also recognize that in today's culture, PTSD can be the catch-all for almost anything. That said, I do know that people suffer traumatic events, and though they may not paralyze them, there are still wounds that will not heal by themselves, even over time. Though I have experienced much inner healing and deliverance, I still feel occasional anxiousness when I hear, smell, or come across key dates that bring back memories of my more traumatic experiences. My hope is that by sharing my experiences, someone may recognize their woundedness and seek the help they need.

For years, I have struggled with my loathing (worse than anger) directed toward my mother. There was so much deep healing that Jesus had to do in my heart before I was able to recognize her inner brokenness. But

Jesus has done a healing work in me, and I see my mother now through Jesus' eyes of mercy and grace.

I wish I could tell you that once you turn your life over to Jesus, all your problems go away. But I know this is not factual. Some of my trauma and tribulations were consequences of my own decisions and actions, and I own up to them. God typically does not intervene to remove me from the repercussions of my own actions, but He does change the way I see things and the way I respond emotionally to events, situations, sights, sounds, and even smells that may trigger memories of past trauma. It takes time because there are often layers of hurt that need to be uncovered, and I am not ready to deal with them all at once.

Some of my trauma has come from circumstances and events completely out of my control and is not related to actions, decisions, or "sin" on my part. Looking back, I do recognize that I judged harshly. I judged myself and my parents for Jeff's untimely death. I know the Church also judges harshly. I have experienced this firsthand.

I urge you, as my brothers and sisters in Christ, to never allow your pride in your "theological" accuracy to keep you from loving those who are inwardly broken and have the need of a savior who binds the brokenhearted. Too often, the Church is unwilling to accept broken people into their fellowship. We are all works in progress. Jesus died for us while we were still sinners (Rom 5:8). We are called to love one another as He has loved us, but so often we see the brokenness in others and refuse to accept them and walk alongside them even as Jesus' transformative work in them is just beginning or is ongoing. Their brokenness can trigger our own issues if we are unaware of the condition of our hearts, resulting in judgment and condemnation. We are called to breathe life into them instead, but the Church will often reject them, effectively speaking death over them, by putting the person in a "spiritual body bag" and shoving them out the door.

* * *

Have you ever experienced trauma in your life? Are there certain date, sounds, sights/colors, or smells that adversely affect you physically or emotionally? Reflect upon your attitudes regarding folks who are broken. What do you really think and feel about people who "just don't seem to be able to get their act together?"

*   *   *

We all react differently to traumatic events. For the longest time, I denied that I suffered from PTSD. I thought only those who suffered from paralyzing flashbacks and either had difficulties remembering the trauma or lived in denial regarding it were diagnosed with PTSD. That was not me. In fact, even when describing my issues in this book, I don't feel comfortable saying I suffer from PTSD. Perhaps you feel the same way. Here is an abbreviated summary of what I found on the Mayo Clinic[3] website:

- Overview - Post-traumatic stress disorder (PTSD) is a mental health condition that's triggered by a terrifying event—either experiencing it or witnessing it.
- Symptoms are typically grouped into four types:

  1. Intrusive - Includes flashbacks, nightmares, and severe emotional distress
  2. Avoidance - Avoiding thinking about or talking about the event, and avoiding anyplace that may remind you of it
  3. Negative Thinking - Negative thoughts about yourself and others, hopelessness about the future
  4. Physical and/or Emotional Reactions - Easily startled or frightened, always being on guard, self-destructive behavior, irritability, overwhelming guilt, or shame

If you are suffering from PTSD and are under medical and psychological supervision, then I would advise you to continue to do so. If that has not been enough, then consider receiving a deep or inner healing prayer. PTSD

---

3   https://www.mayoclinic.org/diseases-conditions/post-traumatic-stress-disorder/symptoms-causes/syc-20355967

is a complicated. It has physical, emotional, and spiritual implications and sometimes has to be dealt with across the spectrum of available resources.

I want you to understand that Jesus suffered on our behalf on the cross. He is not a distant God but is familiar with our physical and emotional pain. You are not alone in your suffering. He is able and willing to receive your pain and suffering if you are willing to give it to Him. It is a supernatural work of Jesus, and He will do this for you if you are willing to believe and trust in Him. If you are in that place right now, then I invite you to use the eyes and ears of your heart to let Jesus bring you into healing and wholeness. Find a safe place and someone who you trust and who has experience in praying over this condition, and together, safely invite the Holy Spirit into your heart, hurt, and pain.

Chapter 6

A New Lie – The Religious Spirit

DURING THE NEXT FIVE YEARS, GOD BLESSED US WITH TWO beautiful children. Our firstborn was a little girl, Charla. Our second born child was a precious son, Doug. I decided I would be the best mother I could ever be. I would not make the same mistake that I had made with Jeff. If I were good enough, I believed God would always keep them under His protection. Charles had given his life to Christ, and we both became faithfully involved in our church. To me, the greatest gift parents can give their children is God, so we made sure our children were raised in the "House of the Lord." Our children were raised on God's word. They participated in all church activities, camps, and any event that had a godly influence. We wanted the best for them and kept them in Christian schools.

Charles was all in with respect to the "prosperity gospel" theology, and up until that point in our lives, there was every reason for it. I had one foot in, but the other foot was still stuck in a "poverty mindset" based upon my life experiences. So, while we were blessed materially, part of me was expecting everything to come crashing down. Even though I was conflicted, not feeling I deserved all we had, when it came to our children, I wanted the best that money could buy, even if it meant making extreme sacrifices. I insisted that Charles do everything physically possible to provide the finances necessary to maintain the lifestyle we had become accustomed to, even if it meant working very long hours and giving up time with his family.

Even when he did come home, he was so exhausted that all he could do was sleep. At times, I know he felt he could never do enough to satisfy me.

After being entrusted by God with such precious gifts as two beautiful children, I started once again questioning the love and trust of my parents. Charles was such a loving father. We loved our children, so why were my parents so selfish with their own needs? Why were their "worldly sins" more important to them than their children? I especially began to question my mother's love since her parents were "ministers of the Gospel." They had been the very people God used to influence my life. Why didn't she care enough about her own children to see that we were raised with a relationship with God?

The more I dwelt on this, the deeper the root of bitterness and resentment came into my heart, but as I always did, I put it aside and pretended it didn't exist. Before I realized it, the memories of my dad's aberrant sexual advances started to surface regularly. I had always been able to avoid these memories, but not now. I was even finding myself watching every move Charles made around our daughter, even though he never did anything to warrant my suspicions. These thoughts were a result of my own insecurity from my past relationship with my dad. I hesitated to let Charla even stay with my parents, but as I grew in the Lord, I began to trust Him to protect her. After all, I was serving Him, and He promised to protect my seed, so I occasionally allowed Charla to stay with my parents.

I continued to raise my family in the ways of the Lord, but I found myself becoming very unhappy and depressed. Nothing could satisfy me. Nothing anyone could do was ever good enough. I wasn't good enough. I always had to do it over and over again. I sought perfection, but it eluded me. I felt like a failure in everything I did.

Early in our relationship, Charles had been my "knight in shining armor." He swooped in and rescued me from my dysfunctional family and my "Danuwoa curse." But the brokenness inside me could not be fixed by human effort. In hindsight, I believe there were some codependent behaviors; Charles' self-worth was, to some degree, based upon his ability to be my "knight in shining armor." But there wasn't anything he could do to save me from my downward emotional spiral. When I was triggered, I would explode, even to the extent of throwing things.

I also started to see in him a behavior that brought out my worst insecurities. As my emotional issues continued to surface, I started catching Charles in lies, but he would never own up to them. Lying brought out all my emotional baggage and feelings of abandonment from my parents, but at this time in my life, I did not understand what was happening to me or why his lies triggered my response. He would lie, and I would confront him. He would deny, and I would explode. This was a repetitive cycle that spiraled out of control, destroying trust.

Charles did everything he could do, but nothing would make me happy. I had gained over a hundred pounds and started taking my self-hatred out on him. I put pressure on both of my children, demanding obedience just because I was their mother. A family and a marriage that were secure were shaking. I became more depressed and more demanding. I began to see him struggle with his own self-esteem. It didn't take a long time for his business to start being affected.

My house stayed a mess. Charles would come home after working thirty-six to forty-eight hours straight, and he would ask me what I had been doing the last several days and would I please fix him some dinner. I replied, "I have been playing with the kids. The house can wait, and I'll fix dinner when I'm ready to fix dinner!" I had become an unorganized perfectionist (Leman, Kevin. 1990. *Growing Up Firstborn*. Dell Publishing: New York, New York). That is a perfect description of me. My house may be a mess, but I promise you my closets are clean and organized!

Charla was entering adolescence, and I felt like every day was a battle of wills. I recognized that we shared some common traits, which I understood was related to our birth order after reading Dr. Leman's book. We were both strong-willed firstborns. I learned that Charla's behavior was not born out of rebellion but was typical for firstborns. I still tried to control her, but knowledge of firstborn behavior did help me get through those early adolescent years with Charla.

I was totally out of control with my family, with my weight, and with money. We were already making house payments we couldn't afford, and now my spending was unconstrained. Perhaps I was testing God and the "prosperity gospel," or perhaps I was testing Charles, all the while feeling my own insecurities and expecting God and Charles to reject me. I know Charles was feeling a lot of pressure.

Watching his struggle caused me to be overcome with self-condemnation. I remembered all the memories of all those I loved whom I had hurt by not being able to be good enough for their acceptance. I blamed myself for all the strife and unhappiness in our family and in our marriage. The self-loathing that began to fester within my heart was unbearable at times. No one but God can help someone who is in my condition. I tried to handle the pain by controlling everyone and everything. If I couldn't control you, I would find a way to manipulate the situations in your life so that the end result would be what I wanted it to be. I would still get my way.

The deeper into depression I went, the more I would withdraw, shutting Charles out. Not only did I need to open up to him, but he was also struggling and needed me to be there for him. I felt I had hurt him enough, and I didn't want to hurt him anymore than I already had.

One evening, I fixed Charles' favorite dinner, pork chops. Charles called to tell me he was on the way home, but he was late. I was furious, and I didn't care what his excuse was. All that mattered was that I fixed dinner and he was over two hours late. I remember very clearly what I said to him on the telephone. "I don't care what your excuse is. I'm sure you're lying to me just to cover yourself. I will tell you right now if you're calling me to try and get in good with me, it won't work. By the way, if you think you're coming home and getting sex, I suggest you find yourself a lot lizard (a professional prostitute who works truck stops) because you're not getting any sex from me!" I slammed the phone down. Charles did not find a lot lizard that evening, but between my behavior and Charles' neediness, the enemy was able to set in motion a plan that led to Charles' adultery.

I don't think anyone is responsible for the sins of another person. They are the ones who have to make up their mind to sin. However, I do feel that I helped Charles make that decision. There was a part of me that thought that he deserved much better than me. So, in a sick way, I was trying to force him into infidelity. Because of my insecurity, I felt he was going to leave some day, so we might as well get it over with. I thought I could deal with the pain that I was going to experience eventually. I thought I deserved the pain and suffering, but if Charles went ahead and left me, he would be free to find someone he really deserved.

We decided we needed some time to pray and seek God's direction for our lives, so we separated for a few weeks. Our children never even knew what had happened. It was understood that we would work through our reconciliation process so that we would get back together only when we agreed to not bring up our issues ever again. When discussing the events that helped to lead us to separate, some of the things Charles said to me were "I tried so hard to talk with you about the problems we were having, and I tried to give you the love and attention I thought you needed. But you would just shut me out. You wouldn't talk to me at all. You also just stopped caring about yourself; your self-esteem, your health, your looks…" I knew how much my weight bothered him, but it couldn't have bothered him as much as it bothered me!

After we agreed to a reconciliation, Charles thought it would be a good idea to change churches. We needed to work at restoring our relationship, and even though we had attended our home church for many years, he thought a smaller church would give us a more personalized ministry. I reluctantly agreed to change churches, but not without screaming and fighting through the decision-making process. I did think that it might help Charles become more mature in God, so I finally resolved myself to the change. I thought that if he grew closer to God, then it would be easier for me to manipulate him. I was more knowledgeable about the word than he was. It would really be a "spiritual" way for me to continue to control him and get my way.

I told him that I had forgiven him for his sin against our marriage, but I continued to beat him over the head with it year after year. If he went to the grocery store and came home with the wrong kind of bread, I found some way to tie that mistake to his adultery. I honestly thought I had forgiven him, but every time I got angry, something would rise up inside of me, and the next thing I knew, I was back to the memory of the pain I had experienced.

Within three months of changing churches, I began to work in the church office. Instead of withdrawing within myself because of my own self-loathing and guilt, I began to use the church as a means of escape. The church and its people became my identity and sense of self-worth. The needs of the church, the pastors, and the people became far more important to me than the needs of my own family. I was out of balance. I forced my husband to make financial sacrifices for the church, even though we were beginning to have serious financial problems of our own.

I became very close to the pastors. They became more of a family to me than my own family. They placed me in a position of great responsibility. I was responsible for all the finances that filtered through the church. This included five different ministries bringing in money. I accepted the responsibility gladly. I was, and had always been, a very responsible person, and I knew I could handle the position with ease.

As my influence grew, I was soon able to control several situations within the church. I had become a person who not only controlled my family but also many of the decisions made within our church. I worked forty to sixty hours a week without receiving monetary compensation. The church was struggling financially, and I wouldn't let anyone know that I could have used the money. Besides, when I quit my job, I promised God I would only use my skills for Him and His ministry.

Being busy doing the Lord's work kept me from having to think about my own issues. Except for strife in my marriage and serious financial problems, everything else seemed to be going great. I had buried all my hurts, and seldom did they ever surface. I had become the perfect "little Spirit-filled Christian." Unlike everyone else, I had no problems. I was just what a "Christian" was supposed to be.

On June 5, 1985, my thirtieth birthday, my dad bought me a heart-shaped diamond necklace. This was rare because he seldom bought me anything. Every time I would wear it, I felt like I was choking. I couldn't forget the memories of when he had bought me material things in the past with the intention of trying to get me to have sex with him. I would take the necklace off and lay it on my dresser, but every time I passed by and looked at this necklace, I would become consumed with anger. Finally, I put it away so I didn't have to look at it anymore.

My parents lived about two and a half hours from our city. Dad was a truck driver, and mom worked in the city. She needed a place to stay during the week while she worked, and then she and Dad would return to their lake home on the weekends. One day, she showed up on my porch with her suitcase and said she was going to start staying with us during the weekdays. My home was my safe place for me from everyone and everything. But Mom moving in changed everything. I started working longer hours at the church. When I came home, I would lock myself up in my bedroom, just as I used to do when I was a teenager.

My memories just flooded my mind. It seemed that I had no control over them. I was angry, bitter, and resentful. I just couldn't get away from the torment of the past years. After several weeks of this, my mom decided to confront me. She was going to make me tell her why I was avoiding her. I refused to be backed into a corner and continued to stay locked up in my room. I was feeling so guilty because I had always spent a lot of time with my children, and then they hardly ever saw me unless they came into my room and spent time with me. I vaguely remember the confrontation with my mom. I had so much anger built up inside of me that I exploded when she confronted me. She left my home in tears, knowing I didn't want her in my home. I was sorry I had hurt her, but I finally had control of my own home, and it was a safe place for me again.

Days later, my mom sent me a letter. I waited three days before I could even open it. The first few lines said, "I don't know what I have done to you to deserve to be hated so much by you. I don't know what has happened to you. You're not the daughter I raised." That was as far as I could read. I threw the letter away. I just couldn't stand to feel any more guilt. Just the comment "You're not the daughter I raised" was enough to torment me. I felt judged and didn't measure up to her standards.

I have always loved God with my whole heart; that has never been in question. My relationship with Him had grown greatly, and my heart was a heart after Him. I desired to know Him in a way that many would speak of, but I knew something was keeping me from entering into His best. I was motivated by my love for Jesus and His people to find His joy and peace, so I began to pray daily and ask the Holy Spirit to create within me a clean heart—to purge me and remove anything that was within me that wasn't of Father God. Little did I know at that time what was going to happen over the next ten years to bring me to the place where my heart could be pure before God and I could enter into His fullness.

Reflections of the Heart

I know that after I recommitted myself to Jesus, I was saved; it was more of a confirmation since I believed in Jesus ever since my childhood days with my grandparents. My eternity was secure. But what I didn't know was that healing or transformation of my inner person does not happen with an instantaneous supernatural conversion. I did not understand that although my spirit was made new, that is, I was a new creation in my spirit, my soul was still tied to my old self. I denied that my old emotional wounds, baggage from past injuries, were still present, lurking in the depths of my soul, just waiting to burst out uncontrollably. As Dr. Charles Kraft would often say, "Many Christians are saved, but they are not free." This was very true of me.

Keeping myself busy allowed me to live in denial. It allowed me to tie my identity into what I was doing and gave me a measure of self-worth that I so desperately needed without bringing about any healing of the brokenness in my inner being. I wore a mask the entire time I served the pastors and the people at church. I even wore a mask at home. I was being manipulated by a religious spirit that was rooted in my woundedness. Perhaps there was a spirit of shame and unworthiness that kept me from submitting to the Holy Spirit, who would have led me to healing and freedom.

Although I believed that I looked like a godly and faithful mother, wife, and steward of our church outwardly, inwardly I was a mess. I was controlling and manipulative in order to ensure that no one would be able to see the mess that I was in on the inside. But control and manipulation are the opposite of grace, transparency, and freedom—all characteristics of the Holy Spirit. Grace and transparency enable trust, but my behavior created an atmosphere of mistrust.

It probably goes without saying, but broken people hurt people. I could not trust Charles or the people at church. I reacted to Charles with an emotional outburst, and he reacted to me by his lying and infidelity. The mistrust at church eventually led the people I served to turn on me, even falsely accusing me of impropriety with church finances. All that just brought back memories of my grandparents' betrayal at the hands of their own church members and the vow I made to never allow God's people into my inner circle of trust.

* * *

When you look at your own reflection in the mirror, what do you see? Do you know the person behind the reflection? Do your friends, workmates, and acquaintances know you deeply or just superficially? Do you hide behind masks in your personal and public life?

* * *

Healing begins with an honest look at ourselves. If you know you've been deeply wounded and are wearing a mask to cover your inner shame, you are prolonging the inevitable. Though you may think that you cover yourself well, your behavior, reactions, and responses to your interactions with people will betray your inner brokenness. Public perception will condemn you because they don't see the hurting inner person, only the outward persona with all its flawed behaviors.

Jesus calls us to be a light in a dark world, but if we continue to wear masks so that no one can see the real but flawed person on the inside, then no one will see the light. Masks block the light. Jesus calls us to be transparent. The work of Jesus as He transforms us brings His glory, His light into a dark world. Let Him bring healing to you, and let Him transform you so that people will see Jesus working in and through you, the real, transformed you. The real person He created you to be.

Chapter 7

Hitting Bottom - Refiner's Fire

IN APRIL OF 1986, GOD SPOKE THESE WORDS TO ME. "I AM GOING to take you through a time of great testing. You will experience loneliness like you have never experienced it before. There will even be times when you are in the presence of many people: your friends, your family, your husband, or your children, but the loneliness you will feel will be unbearable at times. Hold on to My hand and never let go. If you let go of My hand and try to walk on your own, you will fall. You will never have the ability within yourself to return to Me. I will always be here for you, but you will not have the strength to return to Me; you will be lost forever. Just remember, always hold on to My hand and don't let go; I will bring you through this time of testing." After God spoke these words to me, I immediately began to watch everything around me, thinking that every time there was a negative experience in life, it must be the trial God warned me of. As the negative experience passed, I would thank Father for His faithfulness to bring me through yet another test, and I reminded Him that I was still holding onto His hand.

The families and the pastors in our church body had become my life. Everything I or my family did revolved around our church. Being raised around ministry in my childhood, I was constantly reminded by my grandparents of the importance of living a godly life among the people of the church. Never be a burden to them. Always show the love of Jesus in your life. Don't let anyone know about the problems you or your family are experiencing. Image is most important. After all, you are exhibiting Jesus in your life. If He can't meet your needs, how do you expect anyone else to receive Him as their Lord and Savior and believe He is capable and willing to meet their every need?

I began to struggle with some of the decisions I faced regarding our church. I started questioning whether or not I was in God's will. The pastor's financial dealings were not transparent, and the church was struggling financially. His lack of openness regarding his financial transactions created tension within the congregation. Rumors of impropriety circulated. As I prayed, God began to reveal to me that it was His will for me to leave the administrative position I held in the church, but this would mean that I would have to turn my responsibilities over to someone else. I would not be able to control anyone or any circumstance if I resigned my position. As the strife within our body became greater, my devotion to my pastors became stronger. Openness or not, I trusted them implicitly. I saw myself in a position of being able to control a lot of the strife, and thus protect them and their children from hurts caused by the people of the church. I loved both the people and the pastors. If I could mediate peace between them, everything would be all right. I had always been the responsible one who handled everyone's problems, and I was confident I could handle this. When God spoke, directing me to leave, I had to decide whether I would be obedient to Him or loyal to the church and the pastors I loved. I knew God's voice, and I had no question as to what He wanted me to do, but I decided not to leave. I purposed in my heart to disobey God's instructions. My ministry became "ministry to man" instead of "ministry to God!"

I remembered back to the hurts my grandparents experienced while going through a devastating church split. My grandfather had a severe stroke and never really completely recovered. I always knew it was because his heart had been broken by the very people he loved and served so faithfully. My uncle, who had married Charles and me, had been deeply hurt in the ministry. He and his family were very bitter and hard-hearted when they left the church. I have always been aware of the difficulties pastors and their families face. I have tried to minister to the needs of God's pastors and their families. I know of the needs that they have and won't share with their congregation, needs that they tell no one but God.

As my pastors came under attack from the people of the church, they began to question the loyalty of everyone, including me. The very people I had been so faithful to began to question my loyalty and my family's loyalty. They withdrew and rejected everyone involved with the church.

As I sat and watched the pain and suffering between the members of our church and the pastors, I became very bitter toward the members. After months of discord, on June 5, 1986, my thirty-first birthday, our pastors resigned their positions, and the church was dissolved. They moved out of state and broke off all fellowship they had with anyone involved in our church body. I remember locking the doors for the last time and telling Father, "God, I love you with my whole heart, but I'll never serve Your people again!" I turned the keys over to the bank, went home, and locked myself up in my house.

Since I was involved in the church's administration, everyone, including creditors, came looking to me, not only for the money that was owed them but also for answers as to why many of the situations in the church had to happen. They were not the only ones seeking answers; I was too.

I still remained loyal to my pastors and refused to speak against them, even though I recognized that they did not steward church finances responsibly. What made things worse was that some of the outstanding loans were co-signed by church board members and elders. As time passed, the board members and elders who signed off on the loan were held financially accountable. This debt created a volatile situation, and everyone involved was stretched financially. The debt holders were facing the loss of their homes. With the pastors gone, I was left to face the anger of the church members. They were caught in the snare of the enemy, just as I was. In the face of the accusations directed at me, the pastors did come to my defense and state that I had no involvement in their financial dealings, but that did not stop their vitriol.

My husband tried to protect me from all of the hurt and pain. He began to monitor all phone calls and visits from "well-meaning church people" just wanting to find out how everyone was doing, or so they would say. My nerves were so bad at this point that I couldn't even stand to hear someone call out my name. I did not see or speak to anyone other than my family for many months.

As time passed, I continued to withdraw within myself and blame myself for everyone's problems. The enemy would tell me, "If you weren't involved, the church would still be in harmony, and the pastors would have never left. You were supposed to mediate peace and resolve their problems." I know now that this is not true, but at the time, I felt my presence in anyone's life caused grief. My parents had problems because of me; my husband and children were struggling because of me; and then my church had split and closed because of me.

This must surely be the test God spoke of in April of 1986. Don't worry, God, I'm still holding onto Your hand, but I don't want anything to do with Your people. Thank You for bringing me through this time. I felt God was really holding me responsible for the hurt and pain I had caused the people I was trying to help. I would be the first person to tell you of God's unconditional love and acceptance, but the enemy had me convinced it was for everyone else. Everyone except me.

I expected pain and suffering from "sinners," people like my parents and people in "the world". But this was a deeper pain. It was a spiritual pain. The very place I had found sanctuary in was now the place I was experiencing the worse hurt I had ever experienced. I soon reached a place where I couldn't even pray, much less believe that God really loved me. I packed up all the Bibles, tapes, books, pictures, and objects relating to God and His love. I only left out items that were in my children's room, including their Bibles. I kept out one Bible for me to carry to church. I still had to play "Christian," and I couldn't go to church without my Bible! People would think I was in rebellion!

God had blessed me with a great memory. But in my emotional state, it was also a curse. I could recall people and events with great specificity with just a little bit of focus. My brain functioned like a personal computer with an icon-cluttered desktop, each icon representing a person who had impacted me, some positively and others negatively. In my self-isolation, I would roll through the icons in my brain and "click" on the icon of someone who had negatively impacted me. I would dwell on the bitterness, judging and condemning them. When I clicked on the icon of someone who had positively impacted me, I would dwell on their possible motivations. I was convinced that no one ever had good intentions toward me, not even God. I would continue to roll through these icons, wallowing in my bitterness, unforgiveness, and resentment. I never deleted an icon.

As time went on, my nerves became worse. At first, my husband noticed that the hair on my head was coming out in places. There would be areas where my hair would fall out. He asked me about it, and I would say, "I don't know why this is happening. I am as puzzled as you are. It must be my nerves or something."

One afternoon, my children were at school, and a woman who had attended our church told them, "Don't tell your mom I'm telling you this, but I want you to know that God has shown me in a vision that your mother has cancer. That is why she is losing her hair. I want you to know that God is going to heal her, and you don't have to worry!" (This is how it was conveyed to me by my children.) This comment devastated my children. They were still very young—ten and seven years old.

Until this time, I had been able to protect my children from what I had been experiencing. I never wanted them to question God or His faithfulness. I didn't voice my feelings to anyone, not even my husband. We just accepted what had happened and never spoke of it because it was too painful. But now my children were being hurt, all due to my disobedience to God. My children had never mentioned my hair loss, but they were scared, and after their conversation with this well-meaning woman, fear gripped their hearts, and it began to affect them. The enemy had convinced them that I was dying, and they thought that I just wasn't telling them. They thought if they told me of their conversation with this woman, then I would surely die.

After dealing with continuous crying and a severe attitude change in both of them, I was finally able to get them to tell me what was wrong. They began to tell me what they had been told. I reassured them that I did not have cancer, and I realized I would have to seek medical attention just to keep their hearts at peace.

I have always been cautious about receiving the "word of the Lord" from other people. I know that just as there are true "words of the Lord" (which I have received), there are also words that people will speak from the carnal self (which was the case here). In this situation, this woman was used by Satan to paralyze my children with fear. You can imagine what her file looked like in my database of memories. Not only had she hurt my children, but she was also one of the women in our church who had stirred up so much strife, and she did it in the name of God's love.

I knew I didn't have cancer. I knew the reason I was losing my hair was because I was pulling it out, one hair at a time, day by day, but I wasn't going to admit this to anyone—not my husband, not my children, not even the doctors. I certainly would never let anyone know how deeply I had been hurt and how much I was hurting for the people, the pastors, and their children. I was hurting because I saw them allow the enemy to manipulate them, causing their pain and, in turn, inflicting pain on one another. I even tried to hide the hurt from God! Maybe if I could control my relationship with Him, I would somehow be able to keep even Him from knowing how badly I was hurt!

It was after this situation that I decided it was time for me to start wearing a wig. The hair loss had become very noticeable. If I covered it with a wig, people wouldn't be so quick to make comments or ask questions, and my nervous habit would be hidden.

The next week, I went for a physical and told my doctor I was losing my hair, but I didn't know why. After an examination, he decided that it was because I needed a hysterectomy. I was experiencing excessive bleeding, and he put me on a drug (Provera) to help control it. One of the side effects of Provera is hair loss. This was the excuse I needed to cover my nervous habit of pulling at my hair.

Anyone who would pull their own hair out must be insane, and I knew I wasn't insane. I had lived through a lot of trauma over the years, but I never lost my mind. This was different. This hurt was private. I had the right to keep my secret, even from God. He had allowed His people to hurt me and my family. I justified the hurt of the past as the enemy trying to destroy my life. The hand of God protected me through it every time. But these hurts were done in the name of Jesus by the "spiritual" people of His church. My innocent children and I were being hurt by the very ones He had called.

After this, I started reexperiencing the situation of my throat closing. I couldn't breathe or swallow. Some days, it would be so bad that my husband would have to perform the Heimlich maneuver on me so I could breathe again. It didn't happen very often; it only happened when I became emotionally upset.

I continued to keep my children in church, and because I knew I was their role model, I knew I had to continue in church. Someone was always following my example, and I had enough problems earning God's love without leading someone on the wrong pathway, or even worse, to hell. God led us to a church that changed our lives. This church had a strong youth group, and they loved God. I knew I was in serious trouble spiritually. I wouldn't even partake in communion, but my children had done nothing wrong. It was the church they needed. I knew God accepted them and had a call on their lives even if I had messed my life up. God still loved them.

I was usually the last one in the door before service and the first one out, and I always sat in the back of the sanctuary. I used every permissible excuse to miss service without my children questioning my faithfulness to God. I would praise and worship God just like I was supposed to do. I even learned how to praise and worship God in such a way that I kept my mind busy and was so distracted by the actual actions of praise and worship itself that I was able to completely block God from reaching me. I used the actual praise and worship to keep from listening to the voice of the Holy Spirit. I had no problem playing "church," praising God, and carrying my Bible. After all, I was a "Spirit-filled Christian" with no problems!

Little by little, God used my pastor, Roger Velasquez, to minister His unconditional love to me and my family. They knew my family and I had been deeply hurt, and he handled us with the tenderness that only God's love can give. As I watched his life over the next few years, I saw love and integrity like I had never seen them in ministry. He actually lived what he preached. Not only that, but he also taught of that special place where intimacy with God was available. The "Holy of Holies," the place I had so desired to enter with God. He didn't just preach God; he lived in Him!

As several years passed, our financial situation became worse, and my husband really began to struggle with his business. God would bless, and Satan would steal. This cycle continued for several years. With each crisis that arose, I thanked God for bringing us through it. Each time, I presumed that this must have been the test He warned me of and that I was still holding on to His hand, thanking Him for bringing me through.

In January 1987, my dad was diagnosed with ALS (Lou Gehrig's disease). I watched him go from a strong, healthy man to an invalid who couldn't even communicate what he wanted to say. Again, I started struggling with my past memories of him. I always loved him deeply, and I was saddened that we had missed out on so many years of having a good relationship.

He was receiving medical disability from social security, and his health was deteriorating rapidly. He knew he would die soon. He had accepted Jesus as his Savior, but he didn't have peace. He became so miserable that he would beg Mom to shoot him and end his suffering. I'll never forget the nights she would call, screaming hysterically, saying that she had a gun and Dad wanted her to kill him. One night, in a fit, she asked if I would give her permission to do it, but I would not. She then asked me to do it and told me that my dad would be ashamed of me for not doing it. I know she saw me as her only means of emotional release, but I really couldn't handle this. I couldn't handle the guilt I felt she was placing on me. The thought of shooting him myself entered my mind, and if my faith in God hadn't been so strong, I may have considered doing it! After this, I refused to answer the phone.

Dad knew how difficult things were financially. If he died before the last day of the month, my mother would have to return his social security check for that month. As he began to realize it was time for him to release his life, he insisted that my mother buy a clock with large red numbers so he could watch the time. He spent three days sitting in his wheelchair or lying in bed, doing everything he could to keep from falling asleep. If he fell asleep, he knew he would never wake up again. He knew if he died before midnight on May 31, my mom would have to give the social security check back. Right after it had passed midnight on May 31, 1988, Dad had my mom call for an ambulance to take him to the hospital.

He was ready to die and didn't want to leave the memories of him dying in their home for my mother to live with later. I received a call from the hospital. It would take me three hours to get to where he was hospitalized. He wanted me to come, and I knew he wouldn't die till I got there. I walked into my dad's room and spent a few minutes talking with my mom. As we watched my dad's face and listened to his breathing, we became aware that he was exhaling his last breaths. I walked over and laid my hands on my dad. I remember how I had trained myself not to get too close to him so he couldn't touch me. I prayed for God's peace, and as I did, he took his last breath and went home to be with the Father. I had never laid hands on anyone when they died. I actually felt his spirit leave his body and then leave the room.

My mother was led out of the room, but I stayed behind to say one final word to my dad. I said, "Dad, all is forgiven. I am sorry life had so much pain for us, but I want you to know how much I have always loved you." I finally realized something through his own actions and his strong will not to die before June 1. He really did love his family. He loved us so much that he didn't want us to suffer any more financial difficulty than we were already suffering. I realized that he had always loved us, and for the first time in my life, I realized that he really didn't remember the times he had tried to molest me. Maybe he was really sick, and the migraine headaches must have been responsible for some of his actions.

On June 5, 1988, my thirty-third birthday, we buried my dad. On the way to the cemetery, Mom mentioned she had forgotten it was my birthday. The way I saw it, there was no better gift I could have received than knowing my dad was with Jesus. It was a day to celebrate, not only my birthday but also his homecoming.

Dad didn't have many material things to leave his children, but he left me his heart. He left me his sense of humor and all of his outdoor Christmas decorations. The year before he became ill, his house was written up in the local papers for its Christmas décor. Now, when I decorate my house for Christmas, I don't do it just for holiday cheer. I do it in remembrance of my dad's love for me and as a testimony to the unconditional love and acceptance that my Father God has given to me. I decorate as a testimony to the forgiveness God offers us, his children, and equips us with the ability, through the Holy Spirit, to offer His unconditional love and forgiveness to those who hurt us so deeply. In doing this, I know my Fathers' hearts are well pleased, both my earthly father and God, my Heavenly Father.

In 1991, our business hit rock bottom. We lost our home and just about everything we owned. We went from living in a 2,500-square-foot home with three bedrooms, four bathrooms, a library/office, and three car garages to a motel with all of our belongings in a mini storage. Stress had become an overbearing, constant companion. Our family name became a synonym for stress.

It was at this time that I had to have emergency surgery. Not only had we lost everything, but now, after having a hysterectomy, I had lost my excuse for my hair loss, but that was okay. I would soon find another doctor who would provide another reason for it.

While I was in the hospital, I was diagnosed with diabetes and put on insulin. My doctors said they were sure the reason I was losing my hair was because I was a diabetic, and after taking insulin for a while, my blood sugar would stabilize. They were sure hair growth would return. That sounded good to me, so diabetes became my excuse for hair loss.

As for the problem with my throat closing, it was getting serious and more frequent. Living in a motel room with an eleven-year-old, a fourteen-year-old, my husband, and a spoiled dachshund certainly escalated my emotional distress. It was difficult enough when I was well, but I had just been released from the hospital after having major surgery.

God is so faithful. Even after all our mistakes and sins, He began to rebuild our lives one more time. My husband's business took a turn around, and we were able to move into a house and live as normal "Christian" people. But I continued my pattern of controlling everyone around me as I also continued to withdraw emotionally.

The most important things in our lives were our children. No matter how difficult things got, we still had our family. A "woman of God" told me years ago that it was my responsibility as a mother to guard my children's hearts and not let anything evil enter in. What started out with the pure motivation of a mother's heart, mixed with bitterness and unforgiveness, soon became a judgmental attitude. As I thought of guarding their hearts, I began to judge the friends my children were associated with, monitoring every action or move they made. I had used this as an excuse to control them.

When Charla was about fifteen years old, a great anxiety rose up in me for her well-being. My maternal family line, starting with my grandmother, married unwisely at sixteen years of age. Each marriage ended poorly within two months. My mother was next; she also married at sixteen, and that marriage ended in divorce. It also lasted only two months. And of course, my marriage to Jim ended after two months. I was determined that this would not happen with Charla. But my behavior toward Charla was rooted in fear and resulted in an overbearing attempt to control her. I saw a lot of me in Charla, and perhaps that was one of the reasons why I tried so hard to control her behavior. I wanted more for Charla; I wanted her to avoid my mistakes and all my emotional traps that confined and isolated me.

My controlling behavior with Charla eventually led to a fierce confrontation that ended horribly. With uncontrolled rage, I slapped Charla's face, and the look she gave me tore my heart apart. I apologized, but that could not make up for the betrayal she must have felt the moment it happened. In spite of all my efforts to ensure that history would not be repeated, "the slap" was a repeat of the confrontation I had with my mother when I was sixteen. This incident was a transition point for what transpired in the following years.

At age seventeen, our daughter went to college. She was in a good Christian college, and for the first time in my life, in spite of the clashes we had lived through, I felt like I had succeeded in doing something right. My husband and I had raised a beautiful daughter who loved God with her whole heart. Now God was preparing her to follow His path. No matter how badly I had messed up my life, in spite of the mistakes I made raising

Charla, she was walking in God's will for her life. Now I could relax! One successful child down, and one to go! Or so I thought.

Charla came home for a visit, and we were faced with a situation where she decided to be in control of her own life. She decided to leave college and marry a young man she had been dating. We explained that we didn't object to this young man but felt she was making the wrong decision. We told her that if she went ahead with her plans to leave school and get married at such a young age, we wouldn't support her decision. We told her that she would be choosing to leave our home and rejecting any further association with us.

Our conversation became confrontational, and again I became furious. There has always been this spirit of rage that would rise up within me when I was upset or didn't get my way. In my emotional state, I spoke some words to her that I will forever regret.

Ultimately, my hurtful words caused Charla to choose to leave and disassociate from us. I'm sure the words I spoke struck deep within her heart, perhaps even deeper than the face slap. I just didn't know how to communicate my feelings to my daughter. I was so out of control. What I had said was very clear to her, but not what I was trying to say. I felt she was making a bad decision. I had so much pain and hurt inside my own heart that I didn't think I could emotionally stand the torment of witnessing her pain and suffering as a result of this decision.

On October 9, 1993, our twentieth wedding anniversary, our daughter made the choice to walk out of our lives. I realized that day that I had taught my daughter to handle her hurt and pain just as I had handled mine. She was just like me. Upon reflecting on the pain she might have to handle in her life, the enemy struck the last blow to any self-worth I had left. But even in all the pain, I have to say that I admired her for having the strength to get away. I had always wanted to do that with my parents, but because of the guilt they had always placed on me, I could never walk away. I had taught my daughter to be independent, and I always tried to guard against using guilt or blame against her to get my way.

Words cannot express the pain and suffering I saw my husband and both of my children experience during this time. Once again, I continued to withdraw, blaming myself for my daughter's leaving home and for her pain, as well as for the suffering of my husband and my son. I was responsible for her leaving because I could not control the situation. If nerves could get worse, they did. I couldn't seem to get victory in any area of my life, but I'm a Christian. Was I living a victorious life in Christ, or was I still living the lie?

It was time for my prescription to be refilled for insulin, and because my insurance was an HMO, I had to find a new doctor. I just chose a doctor at random, but I believe God had the choice planned. I went to see this doctor, and upon examining me, he gave me a prescription for insulin. Then he asked me about my hair loss. I gave him the same excuse that I had been using since my hysterectomy. I lost my hair because of diabetes. He said he really didn't believe that was the cause, and he wanted me to see a specialist. I panicked for a moment, and then I agreed to go see a dermatologist. I had fooled my family, my friends, and five other doctors. I'm sure I could fool one more doctor if I controlled the situation.

One sin I have always stood firmly against is lying. I don't lie, and I don't appreciate being lied to. I'll always be here for you, but if you lie to me, I'll never trust you again. Everyone I had ever trusted, except for my grandparents, had lied to me and caused me great pain and suffering. In spite of my stand against lying, I was living a life of lies.

Upon visiting this specialist, I was asked, "Do you pull at your hair? Have you pulled your hair out because of nervousness, stress, or trauma?" No one had ever asked me these questions before. Now I was face to face with my sin. Was I going to admit to this doctor and to myself that I had pulled my hair out, or would I do the thing I despised the most and lie to him? I answered him truthfully, and for the first time, I came face-to-face with the fact that I had pulled all of my hair out.

It's hard to understand how or why a person would do this to themselves. I'm not even sure I understood. I was taught not to drink, do drugs, or be sexually perverse. These were all sins against God. I was never taught that self-destruction was a sin. Maybe you chose to become a drug addict or an alcoholic, or perhaps you decided to become involved in a sexual sin, but I chose to destroy myself directly and by my own hands. The negative fruits of bitterness, resentment, and unforgiveness resulted in an inward nervous breakdown in which I pulled out my hair because of my own self-loathing. It was a way to destroy myself without involving myself in a "worldly sin."

As I recall the doctor's appointment, I remember the note he wrote to my physician. "Patient suffers from a nervous disorder called trichotillomania. I recommend she be sent for psychological counseling." As I walked to my car, I prayed, "Father, I don't need to see a psychiatrist for counseling. I just need for You to heal my broken heart.

No matter how hard I tried to avoid it, two verses of God's word would continuously run through my mind. "The heart knows its own bitterness, and no stranger shares its joy" (Prov. 14:10 Amplified) and "Even in laughter the heart is sorrowful, and the end of mirth is heaviness and grief" (Prov. 14:13 Amplified).

When I returned to face my physician with this diagnosis, I asked him what he was going to do and if he was going to make me go to a psychiatrist. He said, "No, I knew the diagnosis all along, but I needed for you to hear it for yourself." He knew this would be the only way I would believe it for myself. He assured me he was capable of treating this condition, and he gave me a prescription for tranquilizers. I was really relieved. Even after he found the problem, all he was going to do was give me drugs to deal with the symptoms. The drugs helped me relax while I continued to pull my hair out. I knew the drugs the doctor gave me were not going to help, so I discontinued using them after two weeks.

I didn't want to continue wearing a wig forever, and I thought I might do damage to my scalp if I didn't stop pulling at my hair. Cutting my hair short would be the best thing for me to do; it would make it difficult to pull. Matthew 10:30 (Phillips) says, "The very hairs of your head are all numbered." I guess you could say that I have been a "high maintenance child" for Father. After all, if the hairs on my head are numbered, then He must have had to recount them, hourly!

The hair pulling was just a symptom of my "self-loathing," and that is putting it mildly. Everyone I loved in life had been hurt because of me. Two and a half years passed without hearing from Charla, and my life was spiraling downward. I became obsessed with dying—not that I was considering suicide but rather that I was looking forward to the freedom from the pain and suffering I was enduring. I had even planned in detail my own funeral, the flowers I wanted, the songs I wanted sung, and even the person I wanted to sing them. I started looking forward to death as an escape from the pain and suffering I had endured within my heart.

In the midst of my anguish and self-loathing, I think Charles was still trying to be my knight in shining armor. We had scheduled date nights in an effort to help our marriage. One day, he brought home a 70s-style blond curly pouf wig. Charles always told me that he married me because of the things I had in common with Dolly Parton (and it's not my singing voice). I think you can imagine what this wig looked like. I was so embarrassed to wear it publicly, but I did. I'm not sure if Charles was trying to cheer me up out of my despair or to live out his fantasies. I forced him to take me to a restaurant on the far side of town to make sure I wouldn't be seen by anyone I knew. Whatever his motivations were, our marriage was still spiraling downward.

Everything was turned upside down. The very people and circumstances I had spent my entire married life protecting my family from were the very people and experiences my daughter was seeking in her life. I had spent an entire life trying to protect my children, and she was welcoming these circumstances with open arms. The rejection of my daughter was more than I could deal with.

In January 1996, I cried out to Father, telling Him I just couldn't take anymore. I couldn't live without Him changing my heart and healing me. It was at that very moment that Jesus said to me, "This has been the test I spoke of in April 1986. Today is the day you decide if you will hold on to My hand or if you will let go, forever." It was then that I repented and begged Him not to take His presence from me. On January 12, 1996, God allowed the person of Judy Taber to die. It was not only a death to my carnal self but also a "spiritual death," after which He resurrected me to a new life in Him. He began a work in my heart and started to prepare me for the ministry session that was to come in future months with Dr. Charles Kraft.

Reflections of the Heart

This chapter in my life was about God putting me through a purification process. I recall the vow I had made to God when Jim, in his stoned and drunken state, had threatened to kill me. I recall how God rescued me from my Russian roulette episode with a drunken Danuwoa, and I recognized God must have had a purpose for saving me. What I did not realize was that "playing church" was not good enough. God wants a pure and spotless bride, but I was not submitted to the Holy Spirit. I still tried to serve Him on the strength of my own will, but that wasn't good enough. God does not allow His bride to wear a mask. Intimacy with Him and masks do not go together. He had to bring me to the place where I was willing to remove my mask and allow God into my deepest wounds, my deepest shame.

The purification process was not and is not pleasant, but Jesus was and is always with me. He never left me. Jesus' path is the path of suffering. He invited me to pick up and carry my cross and follow Him. It was and still is an invitation to join Him in suffering so that I would experience His resurrected life in me. I finally understood that I had to lose everything to gain what I never had. Charla's leaving was the loss that broke me. It broke my heart and ultimately left me in a place where I was finally able to surrender completely to Jesus. But the remarkable thing I discovered is that dying to my carnal self—that is, picking up, carrying my cross, and following Jesus—was far less of a burden than the weight I was carrying pretending to be someone that I was not. I was yoked to a religious spirit—shamed into pretending that I was a perfect and loving wife, mom, and Christian. The truth is that this yoke was a yoke of slavery forcing me to carry my own shame, unworthiness, and self-loathing. Religious spirits added to my burden; they did not take anything away. Every step was painful, and death became my hope and companion.

Jesus allowed me to go down this path of my own choosing until, like the prodigal son, I came to my senses (Luke 15:11–32). The difference between me and the prodigal son was that the prodigal son knew he was choosing a path that was contrary to the wishes of his father, and so he recognized that his suffering was due to his own rebellion. I thought that I was a "good Christian"—that I was doing what every other Christian does—putting on the mask of joy, peace, and contentment no matter what I was feeling on the inside. I was probably more like the elder son in the prodigal parable. Neither the younger prodigal son nor the elder son had a relationship with the father that was anything that the father would have liked. Both were suffering from a broken relationship with their father. Both needed to come to their senses in order to be reconciled to their father. This parable ends without providing closure with respect to the elder son. We are left to imagine whether or not the elder son comes to his senses.

* * *

Have joy and peace been fleeting no matter how much you have strived to attain them? Have you been suffering on the inside? Do you know the intimacy that comes from truly being one with Jesus and Father God through His Holy Spirit?

* * *

You may be going down a path of your own choosing and experiencing the same pain as the prodigal son because of your rebellion. Or perhaps you are suffering even though you have been loyal to Father God, or thought you have been—much like the suffering of the elder son in the parable and much like me. Whether you are suffering out of rebellion or out of your own self-righteousness, Jesus has the same hope and words of encouragement for you.

To you, Jesus says: "If anyone should come after me, let him deny himself, take up his cross and follow me" (Matt. 16:24). Jesus invites you into His suffering and His death. But He tells you that His "yoke is easy and his burden is light" (Matt. 11:30). When you deny yourself, pick up your cross, and follow Him, he helps you. When you willingly put on His yoke, He is the burden-bearer. Your burden is light because He carries the bulk of the load. He invites you into His burden and into His death because He gives you His resurrected life in exchange. You are trading your death for His, but His death comes with a resurrected life. It's through His resurrected life in you that you experience joy and peace, regardless of your circumstances. If you have not experienced His joy and His peace in your life, then I invite you to do so now by praying this prayer with me:

Lord Jesus, I confess that I have done things my way. I have chosen what I thought was best for me, but my way has not yielded the joy and peace in my soul that I desire. I confess that I fear choosing to surrender my will to You. Trusting in You and Your goodness in all things has been difficult, but, Lord, I come to You today in this moment, and I surrender my will to You. I say to You, 'Not my will but Your will be done.' Help me in my weakness to trust You in all things. Open the eyes and ears of my heart so that I can see You and hear You. Help me to know you more fully and intimately. Lord Jesus, please break the yoke of a religious spirit that binds me to my self-righteousness. Break my yoke to the spirit of shame that tells me that I should not allow anyone to see the real me, even in my brokenness. Break the yoke of unworthiness, hopelessness, and death wish that oppresses me and leads me to loneliness and death. Lord Jesus, I chose You. I chose to be yoked to You and nothing else. I submit my will to You and only You. Amen.

Chapter 8

Resurrection

As each day passed, something new would happen in my life. I thank God daily for my pastors. They accepted me and loved me even though I was very unlovable. They never criticized me; they just loved me and prayed for me. They were always there when I needed them.

Over the next few months, God orchestrated several events in my life. I knew He was doing a great work in me, but I also knew that I still had this nervous habit of pulling at my hair. I would pray and ask Him to heal me, then my hair would grow some, and then I would pull it out again. The episodes with my throat were beginning to happen several times a week and sometimes several times in one day. One afternoon, I had an episode at work, and I didn't think I would start breathing again. One of my coworkers realized what was happening and immediately did the Heimlich maneuver on me. She knew she didn't even have time to get the nurse. I started to pass out and would have had she not immediately responded.

Pastor Velasquez began teaching about having a "Dialog with God" through prayer journaling. I started my prayer journaling discipline immediately thereafter. This allowed me to open my heart up to God in a way I never could before. I started sharing things from my heart with Him—things I didn't even know were there, things buried deeply. It had given me a newfound freedom in Him—a means of telling Him my deepest desires and secrets, secrets I couldn't share in normal times of prayer with Him.

During praise and worship, I have experienced the presence of God, but I knew there had to be more. What about this great, unconditional love people spoke of? God, if You really loved me, why wouldn't You allow me to enter the Holy of Holies? I did not feel unconditionally loved. How could He love someone who hated themselves as much as I did? Not only that, since I had pulled my hair out, did that mean that I had lost my spiritual covering?

After experiencing God's powerful anointing in a service, I would leave church and find myself asking God, "Is this all there is to You? I'm supposed to live a victorious life in You, but I don't feel it. If You are my strength, why can't I stop pulling out my hair? I must not be worthy of Your healing grace. I must have sin in my life that keeps me from You, but I am a "good Christian." I'm what the "church" expects me to be.

I have had many "well-known" ministers pray for my healing, and I have had many "only God-known" ministers pray for my healing. Benny Hinn has been one of the only evangelists that I have been able to receive the teaching of God's word from. I am a covenant partner and have attended many of his crusades. In July, I was honored to be able to attend a Partner's Conference in Dallas. The services were the most powerful services I have ever been in. The move of the Holy Spirit cannot even be explained. My life was dramatically changed. He anointed each person and prayed over each of us. I experienced the presence of God in a way I'd never experienced before. But even after these services, I went away asking God the same question. I'm tired of playing "Christian." There must be more to you, God. I see people being healed and lives being changed, but I'm still here asking the same question! God, isn't there more to You than this, and what have I done that was so bad it would keep me from entering Your Holy of Holies? I have cried and pleaded with God to do something that would allow me to stop this nervous habit. I would tell Him, "If you're not going to heal me, just allow me to come home." Nothing has stopped the irresistible urge to pull at my hair, and now, even after these powerful anointed services, I'm walking away without any relief from this incessant impulse to grab, twist, and pull!

It was at this point that I started to experience something new. On many nights, after an intimate encounter with Father God, Jesus, and the Holy Spirit, I would have terribly embarrassing sexual dreams. It was always after I had been asleep for some time. I would start dreaming of different beings approaching me in my sleep, desiring to have sex with me. I have to say I have hesitated about sharing this with anyone, much less everyone who is reading this. However, after I heard several women talking about similar experiences, I decided that I needed to expose this area that the enemy must use quite often on women, though no one wants to talk about it. Sometimes, in these dreams, there were people I knew, but there were many different names and faces—people I have never met. Some nights, they would be so tormenting that when I woke up, I would have to look around just to make sure I hadn't had sex and didn't remember it. I was aware of the sexual perversion that ran in my family's bloodline, and so I always guarded my heart and mind from this temptation, but it seemed that when I would have these dreams, I would have no control over them.

This increased the guilt I would feel when drawing close to Father God. I began to think there must be something terribly wrong or sinful with me because I couldn't seem to stop these dreams from happening, and the closer I would draw to Father, the more intense they would become. I convinced myself I was continuing in some unknown sin because even though I would confess and repent of everything I knew, these dreams would come right back. It couldn't be demonic because I am a "Spirit-filled Christian." We can't be demonized. It must be me!

In October 1996, I heard a promo on the Trinity Broadcast Network (TBN) regarding a seminar that was being hosted by a Bible college in our local area. The speaker would be Dr. Charles Kraft, and the subject would be "Spiritual Warfare." I remembered hearing the name Dr. Charles Kraft before. The first time I heard it verbally was when he was mentioned by Sharon Daugherty in a worship service in a Bible class taught by her and her husband. I had a special interest in meeting him because prior to this worship service, the Holy Spirit impressed upon me in a non-verbal manner that I would be involved in international ministry with "Charles Kraft." It happened while I was prayer walking through a neighborhood, evangelizing door to door. I laughed it off originally, but of course, verbally hearing the name from Sharon Daugherty's lips and then on TBN, well, the Holy Spirit definitely had my attention.

I immediately called and inquired about the seminar and found out that it was part of an accredited class at a Bible college and there was a fee of $3500, which was beyond my ability to cover. However, a couple days later, I received a call back, and because the registration was low and space was available, they would give me a reduced rate ($500) to audit the class. I had recently quit my job and still didn't have the money, but I felt compelled to take the class. I have always studied everything I could get my hands on concerning "spiritual warfare and prayer," and I was really excited that a man of Dr. Kraft's credentials would be teaching me and challenging me to learn more in this area. The seminar would be held over a three-day period. Each day would provide ten to twelve hours of teaching and ministry on the subject of spiritual warfare.

As the time got closer for the seminar, the enemy did everything possible to try to discourage me from attending. Some of the thoughts I had were, "*I really can't afford to spend the money,*" or "*I'm really too busy to spend this much time on spiritual warfare,*" and the best one yet was, "*You better check this out with your pastor. I bet he wouldn't approve of this seminar.*" My mind was flooded with excuses for not attending.

As I entered the room for the first session, I saw this quiet gentleman, probably in his early sixties, standing quietly at the front of the room, preparing to teach this seminar. I always sit as close as possible because I like to have close eye-to-eye contact. I want to look directly into the speaker's eyes so I can discern if he is really speaking the truth. So, I took my seat. I sat on the first seat on the inside of the second row, right in front of Dr. Kraft.

Dr. Kraft began to instruct us on his style of teaching and spoke of how he related "spiritual warfare with inner healing." I thought, *What have I gotten myself into? I don't remember anything being said about inner healing, and I didn't pay money to hear about inner healing.* I was an intercessor and knew that I didn't need it. To make matters even worse, I was in a room full of "ministers of the Gospel!"

I have the highest respect for ministers and pastors—or so I thought—but I realized that I had become bitter towards many of them through my previous experiences with our church. I have always admired and respected the call God has placed upon their lives, and I know this is the highest calling of all, but for some reason that day, I began to feel threatened by just being in the same room with them. So now I had to face reality. I paid money to attend a seminar on "inner healing" disguised as "spiritual warfare," and I was going to have to sit through it for not only three days, which equaled over thirty hours of teaching and ministry time, but worse yet, I had to be surrounded by "Men of God" who thought they knew more than the person teaching the seminar.

As I listened to Dr. Kraft speak, I continued to battle all the negative thoughts that hammered away at my mind. I have to analyze everything I hear. So, I took each sentence he spoke, considered it, analyzed it, and judged it. I organized my thoughts into three categories: *I don't think I agree with him*; *I'm going to have to check this out*; and *I don't know if he has a biblical basis for what he is saying.* Dr. Kraft taught a morning session, an afternoon session, and an evening session. The evening session consisted of ministry to those who would volunteer. I decided that since I was there, I would just make the most of it. At least I could rejoice in the fact that I was knowledgeable enough in "The Word" not to be deceived by this man.

During first evening's ministry time, Dr. Kraft ministered to a young man who was the first volunteer. He was severely overweight and had to deal with the rejection that came with his weight. My heart was moved with such compassion as this young man spoke of the inner pain he had been carrying over the years. As he spoke, tears ran down my face. I could taste the saltiness of my own tears as they ran past my lips. Some of the things he was saying were the very things hidden so deeply in my heart.

Deliverance has always been a part of the training I have received in years past, but Dr. Kraft's deliverance was uniquely different. My training and experience in deliverance could be described as hard core, harsh yelling, and screaming. Deliverance was always for the sinner, not the Christian. I would always question God, "Where is the love for this person?" I never want to exalt a man or his ministry, but as I watched Dr.

Kraft, an unconditional love and a supernatural compassion flowed through him. He handled each volunteer as I felt Jesus would have handled them. It was as if Jesus Himself were sitting in the chair instead of Dr. Kraft. I could no longer question the integrity of this man. I could question his theology, but I couldn't question his motives or the love and compassion I saw in him. This could only be the love and compassion of Jesus operating through him.

On my drive home, I had many questions about the session with this young man. There was definitely demonization, and he had been held in captivity for a long time. As Dr. Kraft ministered, these demons would manifest. Dr. Kraft would ask the Holy Spirit for direction, and then he would begin to take this man through the process of inner healing, beginning at the time of conception, allowing him to see that he was really the person that God had created him to be. Could it be demonization that holds so many of us in the "church world" captive, never allowing us to reach "fullness in Jesus"? Is this why I have been unable to live a victorious, undefeated life? I wanted that victorious life, a life Dr. Kraft describes as "Christianity with Power!"

Up to now, all my experience with deliverance was verbally loud and confrontational. It was often accompanied by violent reactions, such as growling, throwing up, humiliation, and physical exhaustion. Was this quiet deliverance of power real? There weren't any "antics" of the hard-core style, which was always showy and sometimes even pretentious.

When I got home, I immediately called Pastor Velasquez to tell him what I had learned and seen that day. Pastor Velasquez walks in the wisdom of God, and I value his opinion second only to God's word. As I explained what I learned, I asked him if he thought I was into something off the wall or if he agreed with some of the things I had told him that had happened. Even though I can't remember his response verbatim, he indicated that it seems to be in line with God's word. Although Pastor Velasquez was not familiar with Dr. Kraft himself, he was familiar with Fuller Theological Seminary and some of its associations. He recognized that there are some areas that he may not be in total agreement with, but he respected the integrity of the ministry that Dr. Kraft is associated with. Ultimately, he said to "judge it by the Word of God."

The next morning, I was anxious to get to the seminar. I took my usual seat and decided I would really analyze this man. I watched his every move and took detailed notes so I could search the scriptures to make sure what he was saying was supported by God's word. After he had started the morning session, he stopped to pray. Again, I cannot remember the words he spoke verbatim, but the gist of it was this: he was feeling led to pray for those of us in the session. He prayed for protection for us and our families. He asked the Holy Spirit to be present and to direct us. Then he spoke to any evil spirits in the room. He bound them to prevent them from causing confusion, and then he forbade them to speak to our minds in the first person. He commanded them to only speak in the second or third person. They could not speak using "I" when they were trying to interfere. Dr. Kraft ended his prayer and then began to teach.

As he taught, I earnestly listened and continued to take notes as I had before. After a lunch break, I looked down at my notes and realized there had been a change in my thought patterns. I was not analyzing him as I had before. Instead of thinking *I don't know about this* or *I don't know if he's in line with God's word*, my thoughts changed to the second and third person: *You really don't believe he knows what he's talking about, do you?* or *You do know this man is way off balance, don't you?* or *You know, you had better check this out—Pastor will tell you that you're in over your head this time!*

Suddenly I realized all the thoughts I had been having were not my thoughts after all. I had always guarded my mind against the enemy's attack, but could these thoughts I had been having in the first person have been thoughts from the enemy and not my own? What about other thoughts I have had in the past when I would continuously blame myself for everyone else's problems? Could this have been a lie of the enemy? Because the thoughts were in the first person, I always presumed they were my own thoughts. After all, "I'm a Christian, and the Holy Spirit dwells within me." How could these thoughts have been so destructive if the Holy Spirit was in my life? And what about the tormenting sexual dreams? We all know that evil cannot be present where the presence of God dwells.

All during this time, I had been praying that the Holy Spirit would reveal the truth to me. I had prayed that He would purge and purify my heart in a way that only the Holy Spirit can do. We took a lunch break, and I spent my time praying for God's understanding and wisdom. I came to realize that it had been demonic influence speaking to my thoughts and that I really hadn't approached Dr. Kraft and his ministry with an open heart. I repented and decided that I would make every effort to understand what the Holy Spirit wanted me to learn during the time that was left.

During the evening ministry session, Dr. Kraft ministered to a woman who volunteered. She had a neck brace on. Dr. Kraft asked her why she wore a neck brace. She described an event where she had an argument with her husband, who was leaving her. She had been standing on the porch begging him not to leave her and had a fall in which she suffered a fracture in her neck. He took her through inner healing, including forgiving her husband. He finished by rebuking demons and casting them out. Afterward, he told her to remove her neck brace and check to see if she still had any pain. She removed the brace, and the pain was gone! Seeing her go through inner healing, demonstratively seeing changes in her countenance, and seeing validation in the form of the physical healing made me start reevaluating my own life. Could the problems I have with self-loathing, the overwhelming desire to die, the constant criticism and judgmental attitudes, the nervous habit of pulling at my hair, and the closing of my throat be connected with demonization?

When the session was over, I wrote Dr. Kraft a note. I told him I would like his opinion in relation to a problem that I had. I explained that I had a nervous habit of pulling out my hair and that the doctors had diagnosed it as "mania" and asked whether he thought this could be demon-related. I also explained that I didn't want to take time away from anyone who really needed to be ministered to. I was thinking that I really didn't need ministry. I was a "Spirit-filled Christian," and I certainly didn't have any problems requiring "inner healing." My heart was fine. I just wanted his opinion. I slipped him this note and asked him to read it later in the evening, at his convenience (at that moment, he was conversing with another person). I really didn't want to have a conversation with him about it anyway.

When I went to bed that night, I prayed, "Father, has it been Your will for me to attend this seminar? Is this the direction You have led me in so that I can experience inner healing of my heart and heal my nerves? Father, have You orchestrated the events that have led me to be at this appointed place at this appointed time so that Your love can embrace me and minister healing to my body?"

Immediately, I felt someone praying for me, and I knew Dr. Kraft had read my note and was praying not only for me but also for direction on how to answer my question. Could this nervous condition be caused by demonization?

It was the last day for the seminar. The enemy pounded me. First, I slept in, and then when I went outside, we were experiencing heavy downpours of rain. My flesh kept telling me to stay home and go back to bed. I thought, *This is the last day, and you have learned enough. Not only that, Dr. Kraft knows your deepest, innermost secret, and you are going to have to make face-to-face, eye-to-eye contact with him. No one knows this secret except you and God! Are you strong enough to handle the shame of a possible public disclosure?*

The only reason I went ahead and attended the final session was that I knew this time had been "God"-ordained, and to stay home would be deliberate disobedience to God. I had learned by experience what can happen when you deliberately disobey God and I was not going to make that mistake again! I realized that this may be the only chance I would have to finally be free from the strongholds holding me captive.

As I was driving to the seminar, my throat started closing on me. I couldn't get my breath, and I thought I was going to have to find someone who could administer medical attention to me. I was not able to talk, but I prayed within my spirit to Father God. "Father, if it is Your will for me to go to this session, You will have to release me from the hands of the enemy. I can't breathe, and only You can set me free. I remember a prayer that Dr. Kraft used, which I verbalized. If this is the enemy, stop it!" Immediately my throat opened up, and I was able to breathe freely. I made it to the seminar and sat in my usual second-row seat.

Dr. Kraft began his teaching and never once said anything to me about my note. Throughout both the morning and afternoon sessions, I had this desire to find the closest exit and run as fast as I could. I wanted to get away from this man who knew my darkest secret. I was finally able to relax at the end of the afternoon session. Dr. Kraft had never mentioned anything to me, so he must not have read the note, or he read it and really didn't have an answer for me, so I was safe. He wasn't going to address it, and I would just pretend I never brought it to his attention.

At the beginning of the last evening ministry session, I was helping Dr. Kraft arrange the chairs in a circle when he asked me, "Are you ready for ministry?" This really caught me off guard. I didn't want ministry! I only wanted him to answer my question. *Did he think I could be demonized?* I told him that I didn't want ministry, and in fact, when he passed around a sign-up sheet, I was one of only two people out of forty-two that had not signed up for ministry. I told him that, and he said that God told him that I was the person for whom he should pray this evening. I couldn't handle that, and I told him, "I don't know what God you heard, but my God did not tell me that!" I grabbed my purse and Bible and left immediately, running outside into the pouring rain. But then the Holy Spirit spoke to me just as I got to my car and opened the door. He said, "You had been praying for healing, and this is your day for it. If you walk out on Me today, don't ever ask Me for healing again!" I knew I had no choice but to allow Dr. Kraft to minister to me.

I walked back in, soaking wet. I apologized to Dr. Kraft for being so rude, and I was submitting for ministry. I felt extremely vulnerable. Not only was I going to have to let Dr. Kraft into my hurts and feelings, but all these pastors and ministers who represented some of the very people the enemy had used to cause me such hurt were surrounding me in a circle and would hear everything I said! My flesh was crying out, *"Run! You don't need ministry!"* but my spirit knew how desperate my inner being was, and thank God Dr. Kraft was sensitive enough to the voice of the Holy Spirit to recognize this. I was really desperate, though I wouldn't admit it to him or anyone else.

Before the ministry began, I told Dr. Kraft about the problem I had with my throat closing. I thought it might be of demonic origin, but I also knew that when I would get under stressful conditions, my throat would always close. I wanted him to know about it so he would know what to do if I couldn't breathe. I can't explain the love and grace he extended to me. As he began the ministry session, he told me I was in total control. I didn't have to say anything I didn't want to say, and if he got into an area that I was uncomfortable with, I could just tell him, and he would change directions.

Dr. Kraft never mentioned my nerves or me pulling at my hair. He didn't even mention my weight. He went directly for the "root" of the problem, knowing that if the root was exposed and the Holy Spirit was able to heal my emotions and memories, all the other problems would probably take care of themselves. He made sure that everyone knew that if there was a demonic manifestation related to certain areas of my life during his probing, it didn't necessarily mean that I had sinned. The demon could have a legal right to my life through family bloodlines, curses spoken upon me by other people, or self-curses. I had also mentioned to him details of the dreams I had been having. He knew this was uncomfortable for me to talk about, and he never brought it up. He only mentioned that there could be sexual perversion in my family's bloodline.

As he began to probe into my life, he asked the Holy Spirit to direct him in the questions he needed to ask. He commanded any demonic spirits to come to attention and identify themselves in Jesus' name. As I sat there and listened to Dr. Kraft speak, I began to hear my voice respond with answers to his questions, but I wasn't the one giving the answers; the demons were speaking through me, using my voice, and I was sitting there listening to their every word, but I still remained in control. I knew I could stop the conversation at any time. This gave me the confidence to allow Dr. Kraft to continue. Many of the answers the demons gave could only be confirmed by me. They recalled specific events or circumstances exactly as they had happened.

As he commanded the spirits to attention, there were many who manifested. Some of the strongest spirits were those of self-loathing, compulsive control, death, deception, shame and guilt, and a head Native American spirit. He asked the spirit of death how many times he had tried to kill me. The spirit replied, "Twenty-five times," and said that he almost succeeded in January. If you remember, I spoke of dying a death to self and a "spiritual death" on January 12. The intention of the enemy was to cause my physical death, in which he almost succeeded, but Jesus stepped in and protected my life. Dr. Kraft asked the spirit of death, "Who does Judy belong to?" He immediately replied, "She belongs to Jesus." "Control" spoke of my need to control people, and the "spirit of blame" told how he convinced me to blame myself for the problems and hurts of the people I loved. When Dr. Kraft addressed these spirits, he prayed and asked the Holy Spirit to make the spirits answer truthfully, saying that I needed to know the truth about situations that had hurt me so deeply. "Spirit of blame" also spoke of how I blamed myself for my daughter's leaving and how he was going to use that hurt to destroy my life. He had convinced me that the pain and suffering my husband and children went through was my fault and that they would be better off if I wasn't in their lives. He had also convinced me that the only way I would be free from pain was to die. As I mentioned before, when addressing the spirit of death, he said he had tried to kill me twenty-five times, but he couldn't succeed. Dr. Kraft asked him why he couldn't succeed, and he answered, "He wouldn't let me." Dr. Kraft asked who "he" was, and the spirit replied, "Jesus wouldn't let me have her. He wouldn't allow me to cross the bloodline." I remembered that my grandparents prayed for me every night before bed, applying the blood of Jesus all around me to protect me and keep me safe. No one knew that but me.

During this time, my throat began to close. Dr. Kraft realized that death was not letting go, so he gently placed his hand on my throat and commanded the spirit of death to release me in Jesus' name. My throat immediately opened back up, and I was able to breathe freely. Dr. Kraft asked the "spirit of death" what gave him the legal right to try to kill me by closing my throat. He replied, "She was born with the cord wrapped around her neck." Dr. Kraft asked, "What do you think about Judy attending this seminar?" Death replied, "I knew who you were (Dr. Kraft), and I tried to tell her she was getting in over her head, but she wouldn't listen!" When confronting the spirit of sexual perversion, which had been passed down through my parent's bloodline, Dr. Kraft asked him (though demons do not have a gender, the voice was masculine) if he had a legal right to my life other than that of a generational curse. He answered, "I've tried to get a hook in her, but I can't touch her because she always stops and talks to that spirit." Dr. Kraft asked, "What spirit?" (He was thinking it was a familial spirit.) When the demon responded that this spirit was my "best friend, the Holy Spirit," I was startled! While the words came out of my mouth, this is not the way I think or speak. I was taught that prayer is a conversation with God and that the Holy Spirit is a friend and counselor, but I would not verbalize or describe my interactions in that way and most certainly would not speak in a masculine voice!

After hearing these statements made by demons, my faith was strengthened. Knowing that these demons knew they couldn't get me to sin because I talk with my friend, the Holy Spirit, built my confidence and reassured me of my faith. I finally realized that many of the thoughts and feelings I had experienced for years were not because I was a sinner, not deserving of God's love, but because I had become demonized in many areas of my emotions and my memories. I was not possessed by demons because God himself dwells within me, but I had allowed doors to open through unforgiveness, bitterness, and resentment and also continued to have open doors because of generational curses that I had not broken by the power of the Holy Spirit within my life. I was demonized!

Another strong spirit was a "head Native American spirit" that identified himself as a "wandering spirit." He had a legal right due to a generational curse. When Dr. Kraft questioned him, he began to reply in a Native American dialect. Dr. Kraft quickly commanded him to speak only in English so that we could understand him. When addressing a spirit of witchcraft, it confirmed a curse that had been placed on me by a witch, and then he gave the name of the witch. Dr. Kraft immediately sent the curse back to the person, speaking blessings on them in Jesus' name. There was also the spirit of the infirmity of diabetes, which was of generational origin. A "religious spirit" manifested. This spirit claimed to be a generational spirit with legal rights through my grandfather's bloodline. He said he had been successful in perverting many of my grandfather's children and family members but couldn't influence me. He said I knew the word of God and broke away from the control of the "religious spirit." When the spirits refused to respond to Dr. Kraft's commands, Dr. Kraft would ask the Holy Spirit to administer pain and torture to the demons so they would respond. The session was so relaxing that after a while, it even became comical at times. I found myself in tears of pain, but soon they were replaced with tears of laughter and healing. After about two and a half hours of ministry and after Dr. Kraft released me from my demonic tormenters, he ended the session. I can't begin to tell you how this has changed my life.

I realized that up to this point, my life was a lie. I was an actor on a stage playing the role of "Judy," but it was not the real Judy. I was role-playing for the audience to meet their expectations of "Judy," but that role was impossible to play. I wasn't that "Judy," and she wasn't the "Judy" God created and had a noble purpose to be fulfilled. God was calling the real Judy to stand up and tell of the healing that God has brought to my inner being and how he has brought me to a place of freedom that I have never known before. His love overcomes me, and His compassion consumes me.

All my life, I tried to be the daughter my parents wanted me to be, the sister my brothers needed me to be, and the wife my husband expected me to be. I tried being the loving, performing mother my children so desperately needed me to be, the friend my friends required me to be, and the employee my employer demanded I be. I tried to be the perfect "Christian" that I felt the church molded and expected me to be. I was never allowed to be the person God created me to be. Now, through "inner healing," the Holy Spirit has brought healing to my whole person. I can be who God requires me to be, the person He has created me to be. I even like who I am!

In the past, when I went shopping to buy new clothes, I had to buy designer dresses in plus sizes because designers had decided what was fashionable for me to wear. One of the most liberating events for me was when I bought a dress that I really liked. A plain black dress with a row of daisies around the neck. I felt so comfortable because I was being myself and not someone the designers had forced me to be. No more large wild florals, bright and bold stripes, and plaids. No more pleats and wide belts. Now I wear what I like and what fits my personality.

How has my life changed since ministry? I have found myself not only loving but hugging strangers as well as "Christians" in my church body. A supernatural peace has filled my mind and my heart. I don't worry about circumstances or financial problems. I don't nag my family like I previously did. Anger and rage that used to fill me with very little provocation have vanished.

I have faith in God that I have trained my children in "the ways of the Lord" so that they have a heart after God. He has them in His hands, and He desires they have a relationship with Him, more than I desire it for them. God will guard their hearts, and He will honor my prayers for their lives. He, not I, will direct their footsteps, and He will protect their lives. I say all this while there is still a heaviness in my heart regarding my relationship with Charla.

Now God has total control of all areas concerning my life and my family. I no longer desire any control other than the control Jesus has given me through His authority, to be used to defeat our enemy! For the first time in over nine years, I invited those God directed me to into my home to share Thanksgiving and Christmas with our family. That year, I invited my mom to join us because I wanted her to, not because I was obligated to invite her and felt that I had to! We may not have been able to offer a lot to them, but we could and did offer them the love of God. I love my brothers and sisters in Christ, expecting nothing in return from them and having faith in the Father that He has led these people across my pathway so that His unconditional love may be ministered to them through my life. The door to the spiritual gifts God has placed upon my life has been opened, and I am freely flowing in them by the prompting of the Holy Spirit.

Reflections of the Heart

It wasn't until my prayer session with Dr. Kraft that I realized how much I did not know about spiritual warfare. I read the Bible, had been to Bible school, and believed in the gifts of the Spirit. Being in a Pentecostal church, I was a charismatic Christian and believed in the supernatural workings of the Holy Spirit. I had firsthand experience with signs and wonders, yet the eyes of my heart had been blind with respect to the invisible war within the spiritual realm over the hearts and souls of humanity. I had no understanding of the relationship between the brokenness I carried in my heart and the influence of demonic spirits to establish strongholds, making me a prisoner of my own mindset. It was a complete revelation to me that demonic spirits were speaking to me in the first person. My entire life, I thought that every thought that crossed my mind was my own. I judged and condemned myself as being a worthless sinner; it never crossed my mind that these accusations were not from me but from demonic spirits.

There was much scripture that I had to review and reconcile with my new experience. I still believe that I became a new creation in Christ the moment I said "I do" to Jesus and His Holy Spirit (2 Cor 5:17), but I now recognize that what is born again (John 3:7) is my spirit. My spirit is conjoined with the Holy Spirit, so not only am I a new creation, but in my conjoined spirit, I am in unity with Jesus and the Father (John 17:21, Rom. 8:9, 1 Cor 6:17). So, while my spirit is made new, my soul—that is, my mind, will, and emotions—is not. I chose to submit to His Spirit—not my will, but your will be done (Matt. 6:9–10, Rom. 8:5). By my will, I submit to His Spirit so that my mind and emotions are transformed and I become more like Him (2 Cor 3:18). This transformation is a process, and that is what inner healing or deep healing is. It is the transformation of my soul, which is why it's spiritual warfare.

Even though I knew I was saved the moment I said yes to Jesus, my identity was still tied to my life experiences. My life experiences told me that I was a worthless fake, and demonic spirits continued to remind me at every opportunity. Though I read in the Bible that I was a child of God, I never thought of myself in that way or lived my life out of that reality. Even though I was saved, I was not free. I pretended to be something I was not because God's transformative work within my soul—that is, the inner healing of my soul—had not even begun until the day I met Dr. Kraft.

I am now living more out of my identity as a child of God than my identity forged by my life experiences. I feel love and joy deep in my heart ("The Holy of Holies"), and I feel the oneness with Jesus and Father through His Holy Spirit. I recognize and walk in my role as a member of the royal priesthood (1 Pet. 2:9) in authenticity rather than faking it. I no longer live as a powerless Christian. I have come to recognize the authority that I have in Jesus because I am His child and because His Spirit dwells in me. But I still recognize that I am a work in progress. Jesus strips away the layers of my old identity over time so that I continue to grow into my new identity layer by layer.

* * *

If you have said "yes" to Jesus, do you live out of your new identity as a child of God and member of his royal priesthood or are you operating out of your own willpower, trying to "fake it till you make it"? Are you restlessly searching for your purpose in life? Are you successful by worldly standards, confident in your standing before God's eyes, or both?

* * *

You may have been born into a "good and healthy family" and blessed with skills and talents that enable you to be "successful" in the eyes of the world, yet you know the restlessness of not finding that inner peace, joy, and contentment that Jesus describes. If this is you, I would suggest that you have not yet found your true identity in Jesus but are working out of the identity that the world has shaped and confined you into having. Or perhaps you relate to my story—feeling as though you are a worthless fake even though you know you are already saved. You also have not found your true identity in Jesus. Whatever your situation, if you feel like you are stuck—that is, you are not becoming more like Jesus—then please consider receiving inner healing or deep healing prayer. Allow the Holy Spirit to heal you and make you whole.

Chapter 9

Working Through a New Paradigm

AFTER MY PRAYER SESSION WITH DR. KRAFT, MY LIFE WAS turned upside down. Since early childhood, I have been aware of the presence of the demonic and have been exposed to deliverance ministries with my grandparents. I remember the yelling and screaming, and people manifesting serpents slithering on the ground. I remember my grandparents picking me up off the floor to keep me away from one such situation and telling me not to look at anyone manifesting because the demons might jump on you. I never thought I would be involved in a deliverance ministry, and I never understood inner healing and its connection to demonic attachments. I never thought that Christians could be demonized, but after my experience with Dr. Kraft, I felt freedom like I've never had before.

I have always struggled with fasting, but after my prayer session, I have discovered the joy of fasting. I've been able to fast and pray for multiple days as prompted by the Holy Spirit. I've lost my compulsive eating disorder. I used to consume up to three bottles of 3-liter soft drinks per day, but now I no longer have the drive to consume soda or caffeinated products. The first forty days after my session, I lost 43 lbs without trying. My blood sugar levels stabilized, and I did not have to take insulin injections. I was able to come off of diabetes medications for over seven years. Today, I do take insulin injections, but my intake level is four times lower than prior to my prayer (and I'm working to get it eliminated again). The best part of all this was that I no longer have the compulsion to pull my hair out. The compulsive desire that would drive me to these behaviors has been replaced with the peace of God. Today I no longer want to die. I love life! Every day is a blessing from Father!

The greatest testimony of what God has done in my life is the change in my heart and the intimate relationship I now have with God, Jesus, and the Holy Spirit. Instead of being transformed from glory to glory, as God's word speaks of, my life had been spent going from torment to torment. No matter how hard I tried or prayed, I felt I could never enter the "Holy of Holies" that I so desired. The intimate relationship that I knew was available to me was not a reality. I always knew there was a more intimate relationship available with God. I've heard people say, "Just climb up in Jesus' lap and let him hold you." Well, I have a hard time picturing me climbing up in anyone's lap, much less Jesus' lap, but now as I pray and approach the "Throne of God," I can see Jesus reaching His hand down to me and lifting me up to Him. He puts His arms around me, lays His head on top of mine, and slowly He dances me around the throne, just holding me and loving me as only He can. He continuously reassures me that I can stay safely within His arms until I am ready to come back and face life and its difficulties. I learned how to draw close to Jesus and stay in His presence until I have the strength in Him to return to face life and its difficult challenges.

As I have gone back through each of my memories, I have been able to see Jesus in all of them. One of the questions the enemy has used to torment me for years was, "If God is so loving, why did He not stop the tragedies in your life?" I just thought it was because He was God, and I didn't even have a right to ask Him. As Jesus took me through each hurt, He showed me just where He was in each situation. He said, "I was right there all the time, waiting and asking you to give Me your hurts, but you always wanted to keep them. They were your private pains, and you shared these pains with no one, not even Me, the only person that could take the pain from you. I could not violate your will, so I could only stand by, watching and waiting, but I never allowed Satan to cross the bloodline that had been applied to your life. He could never destroy you, and I had faith in you that you would call out to Me when you were willing to release all your hurts and pains to Me." After Jesus said this to me, all the questions were answered! I can look back at the past and the people in my life and thank God for His unmerited favor and grace. I am finally able to understand why the enemy was allowed to do what he has done in my life, but he has never been able to destroy me. I am under the blood of our crucified Christ. The memories no longer have any control over me. I have come to a new understanding of what the blood of Jesus has done for me and the power that flows through His precious blood.

I want you to also understand that I did not receive hundred percent freedom with a single two-and-a-half-hour prayer session. That first session brought a great deal of freedom, but I also recognize the ongoing process of inner healing that has continued on in my life over many years. It is a transformative process worked out by the Holy Spirit with fear and trembling (Phil 2:12). There was much that I needed to learn and much that I needed to unlearn.

One of the things I needed to learn was the understanding of what an "inner child" was. Today, the concept is well accepted by popular psychology, but early on in my transformation, I did not accept the concept. I refused to believe that I had "inner children," but over the course of many ministry sessions working by Dr. Kraft's side, I saw childlike behavior exhibited by highly intelligent, well-educated people. I saw the fruit of the healing of painful memories carried by these inner children. These were not dissociative personalities (i.e., the person being prayed for did not have dissociative identity disorder (DID) or split personalities; see Appendix C). What I saw was that when a child had a detrimental experience that remained unresolved, then anger, unforgiveness, and/or bitterness often resulted, which the adult person buried deep within their heart. Unfortunately, demonic attachments were also formed by these unresolved emotional issues. Tormenters with accusing voices condemned and confined the inner child within their experience, causing them to relive it whenever the inner child's emotional response was triggered.

One of my early painful memories that Father healed was of a three-year-old "inner child." The memory was within my cognitive awareness, but I didn't understand the strength of the emotional bonds tied to it. These emotions lurked deep within my heart but would resurface when they were triggered, though I had no understanding of what the trigger was. When it was triggered, I would react as if the three-year-old was still active within me. When I confronted the three-year-old little girl, she wanted nothing to do with me. She kept her back turned to me and wouldn't answer my questions. I asked Jesus to direct me when approaching her. I asked her why she was so upset with me. She answered, "You made me leave my grandparents. They were the only ones who really ever loved me, and you are responsible for all the pain and suffering I have gone through." I quickly repented to Jesus, and then I asked her to forgive me. She forgave me, and both of us together asked Jesus to bring us into unity with each other and with Him.

Sometime later, I discovered a rebellious fifteen-year-old inner child. I confronted the fifteen-year-old teenager, who had been deeply hurt. She wouldn't speak with me, so I asked Jesus to help us with the healing that needed to take place. She felt like I had abandoned her and that she was all alone. There was no one she could trust, not me or my family. Since she didn't know Jesus as the Lord of her life, so she couldn't even trust in Him. I discovered that it was the fifteen-year-old who started pulling her hair out. She did so out of anger and frustration that no one was willing to help her with all the secrets she alone was burdened with. The adult me (forty-something at that time) had a hard time with this rebellious teenager—even blaming her for the trichotillomania. The reconciliation with this inner child was not done overnight. Eventually, she agreed to accept Jesus as her Lord and Savior and allow Jesus to be the mediator between her and the adult me. Over time, I was able to see the fifteen-year-old through Jesus' eyes. Now, I was finally able to understand the overwhelming feeling I had: believing that I was all alone and that I could trust no one! Then I asked her to forgive me. I explained that now she was a "Christian" and that she would never be alone. I told her that Jesus would always be there for her, especially when she felt she had no one to trust, and that since He was in her heart, she would never be alone again. It took some time, but she forgave me, and both of us asked Jesus to continue to be Lord over our lives and bring us into unity so that we could be as He created us to be!

As I have been healed and continue to be healed, the Holy Spirit has made me more aware of these hurting children of God. Father has allowed me to feel His compassion, and He has given me a desire to see them set free, just as He has set me free.

Reflections of the Heart

My heart's cry is for those who have been living the same defeated life as a "Christian" as I have been living. Those who have been molded by society, the church, and their very loved ones into someone other than the person God created them to be. The person who goes to church every time the door is open greets you with their smiling faces and their "Praise the Lord, don't we serve a victorious God!" and yet, they hurt so deeply within their hearts, they may even be trying to decide if life is really worth living another day. Many people disguise themselves as being "super-spiritual" Christians, but they use this as a cover to keep anyone from knowing they are just as human as the rest of us and that they have problems just like I have had. The sad reality of this type of behavior is that they really haven't experienced Father's love in the intimate way that He so desires. They have learned to control their relationship with Him, and they only allow Him to be as close to their lives as they want Him to be. Father's word teaches us that if we draw close to Him, He will draw close to us. Many want Him to draw close to them but are afraid to do so. Spirits of shame, unworthiness, performance, criticism and judgment keep people from stepping into their true identity in Christ. They refuse to open their hearts to Him so He may heal their deepest wounds. Unfortunately, the church is full of these people.

When Jesus was establishing his church shortly after the day of Pentecost, there was an incredible move of the Holy Spirit, but with that move came a divine purging. The story of Ananias and Sapphira (Acts 5:1–11) is quite familiar to many of us, but while the church has grown in number, I think we have lost some of the reverent fear of the Lord that was present in the early days of the church. Ananias and Sapphira pretended to be more than they actually were. They wanted to be seen and identified with those who had truly given themselves wholly to the Lord, but they were holding back. The reality of the church today is that we are more like Ananias and Sapphira than we would like to admit. I know I was. I was fortunate in that God did not judge me in my false pretense as He did with them. But I believe as we get closer to the end, when Jesus comes back for His bride, there will likely be a purging, much as we saw during the beginning of the church. If Ananias and Sapphira were examples of the beginning, how much more purging should we expect at the end?

* * *

Are you still holding things back from God, or have you surrendered every part of your will to Him? If you are still holding back, do you know why? Do you trust in His goodness? And if at any point you do not, do you know why?

* * *

If you know you are withholding anything from God, and especially if you know the reason is due to shame or fear related to your true identity, then I urge you to open your heart to Jesus and His Holy Spirit and allow Him to bring you into deep healing. Let Him into every part of your life and every memory, however deep the pain and shame may be. Allow Him to heal the "inner child" within you as well as the seasoned and crusty person you have become. You are neither the wounded three-year-old nor the reticent senior, or anything in between. You are a child of God. Your inner person has no age as long as you are conjoined to Jesus in your spirit and allow Him to bring you into the fullness of His being in your heart.

Chapter 10

Plunging into the Deep

FOLLOWING MY PRAYER SESSION WITH DR. KRAFT, I ENROLLED in a Bible school to study pastoral care and also started serving in a deliverance ministry in Oklahoma City. The person overseeing the ministry had also been at Dr. Kraft's seminar, and he invited me in to help them learn about inner healing and how it can be integrated into their deliverance ministry. Their form of deliverance was similar to what I had experienced with my grandparents. Yelling, screaming, and borderline abusive. Screaming and yelling at demons is certainly not abusive, but what they did not understand at that time was the presence of the "inner child" or, in some cases, a dissociated personality. I also did not understand, or at least did not accept, these psychology concepts at that time. The inability to recognize the difference between an "inner child" and a dissociated personality can result in verbal abuse and cause more damage than good. I've seen adults curl up into a fetal position while the minister was yelling for the demon to come out when the issue was not the presence of a demon but an "inner child." I do not want to disparage any ministers involved in deliverance ministries as I know that everyone involved in this ministry works to free people, loves the Lord and the people he or she ministers to, and only does what they have been taught and trained to do, all with a good heart and intent.

This was my immersion into the ministry. It was not a slow, incremental wading into the waters, but rather jumping into or being pushed into the deep end—sink or swim. It was like getting pushed off the edge of a cliff. I recognized that there was still much for me to learn before I could effectively teach others. But I also recognized that teaching and training in this ministry were critical to ensuring those precious but hurting children of God could be brought to healing in His loving presence and not be exposed to more abuse coming from the hands of those who are well-meaning and also love the Lord but are not equipped to do this ministry in a safe and loving environment.

I stayed in contact with Dr. Kraft, and within about two years, he invited me to a two-week intensive study at Fuller Seminary in Pasadena, California, on spiritual warfare and inner healing. I gladly accepted. After this two-week intensive, my ministry life exploded. I did not understand what it meant to find favor with God, but with respect to ministry, that is what happened to me. I started to receive multiple invitations to teach on inner healing and deliverance.

My first invitation came from Pam (not her real name). Pam was a more mature woman of Irish origin. She had a PhD from Fuller Seminary and worked at a Bible college as well as other ministry institutes in South Dakota. In ministry sessions, Dr. Kraft would pair people together, and he paired me with her. Pam intimidated me, and she always seemed to be angry with me. I would not have chosen to be partnered with her. She had a dominant personality and was even a little mean-spirited. What I did not know at that time was that she was a former member of the IRA (Irish Republic Army) and that she had a dissociative personality disorder. Pam later told me that I reminded her of her cousin in the IRA. When Pam left the IRA, her relationship with her cousin had become quite contentious. During our ministry session, she expressed hatred toward me and wanted to kill me.

Pam and I stayed at the Fuller Guest House. On the way back from the evening session, Pam was walking behind me down some stairs. Pam suddenly felt two hands shove her down to the ground, though no one was behind her. Her fall was serious, and we had to call an ambulance. Pam was a fighter but looking around and seeing no one there beside me (I was in front), she became intensely aware of someone or something oppressing her. Up to this point, she had not bought into Dr. Kraft's teaching on spiritual warfare, inner healing, and deliverance, but this event flipped her switch to adopting this new paradigm. Pam became a fierce proponent for the ministry. She was the first person to invite me to do a workshop.

Most of Pam's students in South Dakota were Native Americans from a nearby reservation. It was my first experience with folks who were heavily demonized and mostly with familial spirits. Many had demonic "spirit" guides.

In the state of Washington, on Bainbridge Island, I was invited by Ray (not his real name), who also was at Dr. Kraft's two-week Fuller Intensive. Bainbridge was known for its natural beauty surrounded by water and mountains, but that also attracted spiritualists. At that time, it was the second most highly concentrated population for shamans. One person I ministered to with Ray was once a protégé of a shaman who had been chosen to wear the mantel for his succession. During her ministry time, she literally levitated off her seat. This opened my eyes to the power of shamans, spirituals, and witchcraft.

I was invited by Ben, another Fuller attendee, to do ministry in Gig Harbor, also in the state of Washington. Ben was a naval chaplain. He counseled young naval men but recognized the need for healing and deliverance, so he invited me into his ministry.

Following these invitations, Dr. Kraft invited me to help him with a workshop in Zurich, Switzerland. It was my first international trip. From this point forward, I was in full-time ministry. There was no turning back.

Reflections of the Heart

My indoctrination into inner healing and deliverance was not how I would have planned it. That said, there isn't a lot of instructional material for this ministry. I have been surprised by the power of the invisible realm. I had very little understanding of spirit guides, shamans, witches, etc. But nothing compares with the incomparable power and authority available through the Holy Spirit, so I was not fearful. The manifestations were not anything portrayed by Hollywood, but they are real. I have learned that it is important to make sure that in this ministry, you do not go beyond your "legal rights" when engaged in spiritual warfare. I have also learned that you do not give the enemy any "legal rights" to establish strongholds within you, as they will torment you. The "legal rights" that allow the enemy to establish strongholds in you are typically unforgiveness, willful unrepented sins, curses and self-curses, vows, oaths, and dedication to any spirit not of Jesus' Holy Spirit. Generational spirits, which have a claim against the family line, and occult practices, including "harmless" games (Ouija Board, levitation games, etc.), which are not that harmless, can be an avenue through which demonic spirits can attach themselves to you.

It is also important to recognize the presence of "inner children" when they are observed. Not everyone has an "inner child" or at least is not aware of them. An "inner child" is more than a memory of one's youth. It is a memory that is so strong that the person is cognizant of the thoughts and feels the emotions of the younger version of themselves. When triggered, the thoughts, behaviors, and speaking intonations of the younger person are expressed by the adult. But this condition is not a dissociated personality (although depending upon the "strength" of the inner child's personality, it may be diagnosed as being on the spectrum of Dissociate

Identity Disorder). The person identifies as a younger version of the adult—same name, same gender, just younger. When doing ministry, you cannot and should not cast out an inner child. Attempting to do so, especially when raising your voice, is harmful.

* * *

Do you have an inner child (or inner children), a recognition of a strong emotional tie to a younger version of yourself? Have you struggled with an emotion (anger, bitterness, depressive feelings, etc.) that you cannot shake off and that you know is tied to a person who injured you long ago, even after you have forgiven them? Do you struggle with a fear or anxiety that you know is tied to a childhood or adolescent experience that occurred many years ago but has not diminished with time?

* * *

When we reflect on our youth and remember people or events where we've been wounded and yet still have strong emotional attachments after many years have passed, it may be indicative of the presence of an inner child. It is important to understand that an inner child is not a demon, but if there is an inner child, there is a high likelihood that a demonic stronghold has also been established. If this speaks to you and you need help, then I would encourage you to get inner healing prayer from a knowledgeable person who recognizes the difference between an inner child and a demonic spirit.

Chapter 11

New Struggles - Enduring Hope

THE YEAR FOLLOWING THE MINISTRY TRIP TO ZURICH WAS filled with one invitation after another. I barely had time to unpack my bags before I left for another trip. I did not anticipate nor did I pursue the opportunities for ministry that came up. I did not solicit the invitations, and it did cause some envy among some of the Fuller Master of Divinity students who desired to do ministry sessions abroad. Nevertheless, Dr. Kraft continued to invite me to his workshops, in large part because many of the pastors requested me specifically. I believe that it was because I was an older (i.e., mature) housewife, and although I did not have the credentials or professional stature of Dr. Kraft and his associates, I was able to relate to a large segment of the folks who desired ministry. David DeBord, one of Dr. Kraft's associates, called me the "Golden Child" because of the frequency of requests made for me specifically. While I did not fully appreciate nor understand why so many doors were being opened to me, I did recognize that God was opening them.

I went on these ministry trips with the blessings of my husband, but as I grew healthier in my inner person, I noticed something in Charles I hadn't seen before. He became more distant and did not seem to feel that my progress toward emotional and spiritual health was a good thing. Charles would say, "You need me," but as I became less reliant upon him for my self-worth, it did not seem to go well with him. I knew Charla's leaving was a big heartbreak for him. He believed that Charla would come back, but the longer she stayed away, the more it weighed on him. She was Daddy's little girl, and his heart was broken and devastated. I believed that he blamed me for her leaving.

Between the time I received prayer from Dr. Kraft in Oklahoma City and my time with him at the Fuller Seminary's two-week intensive study, I was continuing to learn how to hear God's voice. I thought God had been speaking to me about opening a missionary guest house before I met Dr. Kraft. But I had also heard God tell me that He was preparing me for international ministry with someone named "Charles Kraft." I had a good laugh at the thought of it and assumed it wasn't God's voice as it wasn't a desire of my heart, and at that time, I hadn't yet met Dr. Charles Kraft.

My search into discerning God's voice started a few years earlier. I discovered Mark Virkler's teachings (Virkler, Mark. 2010. *4 Keys to Hearing God's Voice*. Destiny Image Publishers: Shippensburg, PA), and I took a more disciplined approach to hearing God's voice following the four keys he presented. I was confident in the missionary respite house, but my spirit was stirred when I heard Dr. Kraft's name in the TV promo for the three-day seminar in Oklahoma City. As more international ministry opportunity doors were opened, I began to wonder if I heard incorrectly regarding the opening of a missionary respite house? I became more confident that it was God opening doors for me in international ministry. What I did not know at that time was that Charles' business and our finances would continue to shrink. If we had invested in the missionary respite house, we would have been buried in debt.

When I accepted Dr. Kraft's invitation to Switzerland, I didn't have any money. He provided the airline ticket for me, but the day before I was leaving, a terrible tornado tore through Oklahoma City. Charles and my son, Doug, were stuck in the city because a curfew had been declared. The phones were down, but I was able to communicate with Charles by email. He agreed to let me go even though the tornado meant we were not able to meet up prior to my leaving. So, I left with the plane ticket in hand and $2.50 in my pocket. I did not have a credit card nor appropriate clothing, and I could not speak the language. I also had a layover in Tokyo, but not having travelled internationally, everything was a new experience for me. I had told God that if He wanted to send me, I was willing to go, so I went by faith even though I had reasonable excuses not to go.

Problems arose on the first leg of the journey. In Tokyo, I did not know that I could not leave the boarding gate area. Looking for something to drink, I exited and entered the lobby area. Turns out that $2.50 wasn't enough for a Coke in Tokyo. I gave all of it to a young boy at a vending machine so he could buy one for himself. I then found out I could not get back in. Waiting on a lobby bench, I began complaining about the mess God had gotten me into. I was cold, miserable, tired, and completely broke in a foreign country and could not speak the language. In the midst of my complaining, I heard God say, "Sit down and shut up. It's not about you; it's about me." I realize that this isn't King James English, but God speaks to me in the same manner as I speak to Him. I was able to relax, and a short time later, two security personnel came by to ask me about my hapless situation. They spoke enough English that I was able to communicate my predicament. Turns out that if you leave the restricted area, you need to pay a "tax" to reenter, but I was flat broke. After a bit of back-and-forth with other airport personnel, I was allowed to reenter and was able to board my connecting flight.

In Switzerland, I did ministry with a lady who did not speak English. I was informed through an interpreter that she had been having physical problems related to her kidneys. The Lord gave me a word of knowledge that there was a spirit of death behind her kidney ailment. I commanded the spirit to attention in English, and it responded back to me in English, even though the lady did not understand anything that was being said! The interpreter had to translate from English to German so she could understand. My experience on my first international trip helped me understand the calling that God had put on me. This was my first international, cross-cultural, and multi-language experience, and this episode of demons speaking in a language that is not known by the host was the first but not the last time I would encounter it.

Even as I became more confident that the ministry door openings were the move of God and I did everything with the blessings of Charles, our relationship continued to deteriorate. I can look back at our situation and recognize that we had a co-dependent relationship. He needed me to need him. His business continued to face financial challenges to a significant extent and to a degree that I was not aware of. He was always angry, and I felt like he blamed me for our financial situation, for Charla leaving, and of course for all my past baggage and controlling attitude, which I had been working to be free of. We constantly argued. There was no peace in our household. Going on these ministry trips was a respite for both of us.

On top of all this, I felt judged by our church members. They counseled me to not go on any mission trips because my house was not in order. I took counsel with the pastor of our church on whether I should continue with ministry or stop and work on my marriage. After much prayer and dialogue with him, he counseled me to continue as long as Charles blessed my involvement in it.

I continued going on ministry trips, but my relationship with Charles became more estranged. It seemed we only saw each other in passing. When I was home, he was out promoting his business. I did not know what was going through his mind as we just didn't spend any time together until one day when I was leaving for a short ministry trip, and Charles had locked me out of the house and left my possessions in the front yard. My friends came to pack up my belongings, and I left for the ministry trip but did not have a house to come home to. Once I got back, I slept on the floor of my friend's home. As much blessing and healing as I had received, my home life was a mess. While sleeping at my friend's house, I had a dream. In the dream, I saw my dismembered body parts in a large trash bin. I was alive and could speak, but each part was disconnected. In my dream, I called out to the Lord for His mercy, and I saw Him carefully take each part out of the trash and reconnect me, part by part, until I was whole. I told the Lord if He could use the mess that I am, I will go through any door that He opens.

Shortly thereafter, I received a call from David DeBord. David had been running Kraft Ministries as well as a counseling center in Southern California. He knew about my situation and called to offer me a job. I again saw this as an opening from God and decided to take him up on the offer, and I moved to California. There I was able to continue working with Dr.

Kraft and go on mission trips. I saw the Lord's favor trip after trip in the most remarkable ways. I know in my heart that my decision to follow the Lord was validated, but it did not come without continued struggles.

On one of my trips, I went to Israel and became deathly ill. I received incredible mercy and hospitality to such a degree that I knew God's hand was involved in my care, though I did not understand why I suffered so. Dr. Kraft paid for my trip home, and only through a miraculous prayer and the listening posture of friends was I able to make it back into the US. Once in the US, I received unmerited care and support. I received necessary and urgent surgery, and while recuperating and unable to work, Dr. Kraft paid for my rent—for close to a year! I was able to return to Oklahoma City for a short respite. I had a small storefront with a backroom converted to a small apartment, where I occasionally did ministry while in Oklahoma. I was able to stay there. My son, Doug, called and invited me to dinner, and to my surprise, Charles came with him. I was hopeful that with my health problems, he was having a change of heart. But that was not to be. While Doug went to the bathroom, Charles told me that if I died on a ministry trip, I should not expect him to bring me home. If it were up to him, he would leave me on the roadside in a trash bag. In my heart, I recognized that our marriage was over.

Reflections of the Heart

This season in my life was filled with incredible and powerful confirmation that I was finding my purpose in Jesus. I had assumed that if I followed Jesus in obedience, everything else in my life would fall into place. But if everything worked out the way it was supposed to, it most certainly was not the way I expected.

My marriage to Charles hit rock bottom. I did not realize how dark a season it was for Charles. Pastor Roger Velasquez, who had encouraged me to go on mission trips as long as I had Charles' blessings, had confidential knowledge regarding Charles. Charles was dealing with his own secret sins that had nothing to do with me or the choices I was making. Pastor Roger was trying to help him, and he would never violate his principles of confidentiality. Ultimately, Charles chose to go his own way. While I was on a course of spiritual recovery, Charles was headed in the opposite direction. I recognize that God always gives us the freedom of choice, and we choose whether to submit to Him or go our own way. My experience, starting with my deep inner healing with Dr. Kraft, led me to choose to submit to Jesus. But Charles had a lot of pain, and admittedly, I was the cause of much of it. The failure of his business, my recovery and self-worth being independent of Charles, thereby reducing his role as my savior, the pain of Charla leaving, and all the church drama we had experienced almost destroyed him. What was destroyed was his identity as a husband, father, and provider, so he chose to start anew—away from God, away from the Church, and away from me.

* * *

Have you ever felt like you had to choose to either be obedient to God or face the consequences of breaking an unwritten "contract" with someone? An unwritten contract is not a legal document signed and notarized, but rather an expectation for your behavior and/or alignment to a person or people group. When you have this kind of internal decision-making conflict, how do you know if you heard from God accurately? What were the consequences of either breaking the contract or being disobedient to God?

* * *

We form unwritten contracts with our spouses and family members. We form unwritten contracts with the people groups we associate with. These people groups maybe associations with ties to our family, culture, ethnicity, or community, or they may just be folks with whom we share a common interest. The people group would include business associates and most certainly our local church body. When the consequence of breaking the contract is high, then your confidence in hearing accurately from the Holy Spirit must be equally high or higher. Otherwise, you will likely not be obedient to God.

Confidence is something that comes through prayer and your personal history with God. Your history with God should include the healing and wholeness of your heart, leaving no place for enemy spirit strongholds so that you are not deceived. Your history should include thanksgiving for all the memories of situations that God delivered you from and blessed you with. Prayers are really talking and listening to Jesus in the "Holy of Holies," that place where your spirit and Jesus' Holy Spirit are in complete unity. Talking and listening to prayers should also be part of your personal history with God. Resources like Mark Virkler[1] and his *4 Keys to Hearing God's Voice* books and videos are an excellent place to learn how. Between your personal history with God and your prayers, His peace that surpasses all understanding is what you need for confidence (Phil 4:6–7).

Lastly, consult with someone who you trust to speak the truth and not just say something you want to hear. This person must be someone with a long history of hearing God's voice and a demonstrated track record of making wise decisions. For me, that person was Pastor Roger Velasquez.

Chapter 12

Trusting God through Disappointments

I WOULD LOVE TO TELL YOU THAT AFTER INNER HEALING AND deliverance and jumping into full-time ministry, all my life's problems are resolved. But that would not be factual. Prosperity has not followed me, and there are still heartbreaks that are unresolved. I discuss them here with open transparency. I still suffer from broken relationships, but I trust in God that what I have not yet experienced will still work out in ways that will bring Him glory. I trust in Him with the hope that all my estranged and broken relationships will be reconciled, even if it's not the way I could imagine. I can also truly say that in the midst of my suffering, I still carry His joy in my heart.

Charles was my knight and shining armor. He was my rescuer and my hope for all good things. He saved me from Danuwoa, my family, and my poverty. But I now recognize that Charles' identity was affirmed in that role. He needed to be my knight in shining armor. He was the successful head of our household, with two beautiful and loving children, and the owner of a thriving business and beautiful home. He was the model for the picture-perfect American husband and father. But as I started on my path toward emotional and spiritual healing, as his business deteriorated, as we lost our house, and as our family broke apart, Charles' identity was also devastated. While I turned toward God for help and healing, Charles rejected God, and although he would not say this, I believe he blamed me and God for what was happening. We were moving in opposite directions.

About a year after Charles conveyed his message to me about leaving me in a trash bag on the side of the road, David DeBord resigned from Kraft Ministries, and I decided to move back to Oklahoma. There was a part of me that was still hoping for reconciliation. But after I settled back into the storefront apartment, I was told that Charles had been living with his girlfriend for over two years. Legally, we were still married, and that created some financial ties to me and to my involvement with any ministry. Morally and legally, I needed to end the marriage. Upon counsel with my pastor, I filed the necessary paperwork.

As difficult as my failed marriage was, Charla was and is my biggest heartbreak. The issues with my relationship with Charla are long and complicated. It would probably make for a good psychological case study.

In many ways, Charla was a lot like me. Charla and my mother were close. I tried to shield Charla from my mother and her erratic behavior. Neither Charla nor my mother knew the secrets I kept buried. In the years prior to my healing prayer, I had a lot of anger and unforgiveness in my heart toward my mother, and that most certainly colored the way I viewed her behavioral motivations. Charla didn't see any of that. She could not understand why I was so distant and unmoved by any attempts my mother made toward reconciliation. My mother wanted to be my best friend, but I was having none of it. All of this was prior to my healing, and what Charla had experienced up to that point in time was my manipulative and controlling attitude stemming from my own brokenness, fears, and anxiety. I understand that from her perspective, all the issues between me, her, and my mother could and should be laid at my feet.

Even though my relationship with Charla is still estranged to this day, I am proud of her. She had the strength and courage to walk away from our dysfunctional family and stand on her own. At her age, that was something I wish I had the strength to do but couldn't. Though I disagreed with her decision and am still wounded by her absence, I still respect her. I still love her.

Reflections of the Heart

If someone were looking at my life from the perspective of an outsider without intimate knowledge of me, they would probably shake their head and think how devastated and sad my life is. After all, I was living the "American dream." I had a beautiful two-story home with nice and expensive material possessions. I had a loving husband with a thriving business. He was my "knight in shining armor." I was saved and thriving in a local church I attended being in a trusted position handling all the finances, which gave me a strong sense of self-worth. I had two beautiful children whom I recognized as gifts from God. But I lost my house and all my material possessions; I lost my husband and my daughter. The church that I faithfully served shutdown. From the outsider perspective, Judy's "American dream" is dead, and she is pitiful. But while all of that is an accurate portrayal of my life from an external perspective, it does not reflect how I feel in my innermost being.

I can relate to what the Apostle Paul says in his second letter to the church in Corinth (2 Cor 4:7–11, 16–18):

> 7Now we have this treasure in jars of clay to show that this surpassingly great power is from God and not from us. 8We are hard pressed on all sides, but not crushed; perplexed, but not in despair; 9persecuted, but not forsaken; struck down, but not destroyed. 10We always carry around in our body the death of Jesus, so that the life of Jesus may also be revealed in our body. 11For we who are alive are always consigned to death for Jesus' sake, so that the life of Jesus may also be revealed in our mortal body . . . 16Therefore we do not lose heart. Though our outer

self is wasting away, yet our inner self is being renewed day by day. [17]For our light and momentary affliction is producing for us an eternal weight of glory that is far beyond comparison. [18]So we fix our eyes not on what is seen, but on what is unseen. For what is seen is temporary, but what is unseen is eternal.

As you have read through my story, you know that my life has been a life full of sorrow and suffering. Some of my suffering has come about through circumstances outside my control, but I also do not make excuses for having to live through the consequences of the poor decisions and choices I have made. As you have read, I suffered the entire time I lived the "American dream." Outward appearances were not reflective of what was happening in the depths of my soul. It was not until I was able to allow Jesus into my deepest hurts and shame that He healed me and set me free from my performance of being the perfect wife, mother, and Christian. I did lose my life, but in return, I gained the resurrected life in Jesus. I was pitiful when I was living the dream because inside, I was a poor and wretched soul. Now, though I have little to measure by "American dream" standards, I am rich in peace and joy.

I want to end this chapter by telling you how my trichotillomania disorder was finally healed. Sometime after my inner healing session with Dr. Kraft, I still struggled with my hair-pulling disorder. During an intimate "Holy of Holies" talk I had with Jesus regarding my struggles, I "saw" Jesus (in the eyes of my heart) put his head down on my lap, and He said, "Don't pull your hair out. When you feel the urge, pull My hair out." I saw and heard Him in this intimate moment, putting Himself in my place and giving me permission to do the unthinkable. It was at that very moment that I was cured. I couldn't pull my hair out without the image of seeing Jesus in my lap as though I were pulling His hair out. This is the Lord that I serve. This is the Lord I love. Only by the Spirit of Jesus living in me was I set free from my disorder. He has since repeatedly given me peace and comfort whenever I needed them.

* * *

Have you been disappointed in life because your dreams have not come to fruition? Do you suffer striving after a dream—something you really want to obtain—but it just seems forever out of your grasp? For some folks, getting married is the dream. For others, a failed marriage is the death of a dream. Success from a worldly perspective is almost everyone's dream, whether that involves money, marriage, fame and/or recognition, or power and influence. Everyone has something that they think they need to be happy. But what happens when your desires are not met? What happens when dreams die? Do you blame God? Do you blame yourself?

* * *

If you are suffering on the inside, then I want you to know that the healing and wholeness I experienced are available to everyone in Christ. Your personal healing journey may be different than mine. You cannot force your imagination to "see" Jesus healing you; you cannot use the image I received to bring about your healing. But you can "see" and "hear" Jesus with the eyes and ears of your heart. Your inner, or deep, healing will come as you learn to submit to the Holy Spirit. Seeing and hearing Jesus may start out feeling like you are simply using your imagination—and in a sense, you are. The difference is that you use your imagination for the purposes God created it for. When I use my imagination to see and hear Jesus, that is what I am doing—seeing and hearing him. As I do this, I learn to submit to Him, and in my obedience, I incrementally hear and see more clearly what the Holy Spirit is leading me to do, separating my thoughts from the chatter of my own carnal self and, more importantly, the lies of the enemy.

By way of full disclosure, I will have to admit that learning to submit to Jesus and being filled by His peace and joy regardless of your life circumstances generally means that you have to let go of your dreams. Learning to truly pray, "Your kingdom come, Your will be done on earth as it is in heaven," means your willingness to put Jesus first, before your dreams. It is trusting in the goodness of God and that what He desires for you is better than what you desire for yourself.

Chapter 13

Breaking the Spirit of Fear, Shame, and Deception

MY LIFE HAS BEEN ANYTHING BUT PEACE AND TRANQUILITY. I have struggled with nervous disorders resulting from having to keep family secrets and trying to bear everyone's burdens. I have struggled with living up to expectations, especially those in the church. I have struggled with failed relationships and particularly painful breakups with my daughter and my husband. I have struggled with failed dreams and expectations of a happily ever after life. And yet, through all these struggles, I now know what it means that "in all things we are more than conquerors . . ." (Rom 8:37). Shame and deception have been the root of much of my distress and disorder, but both have been broken and I have been set free.

Dr. Kraft was on the board of C. Peter Wagner's Leadership Institute (WLI). At that time, the Leadership Institute met in Colorado Springs and held conferences. Dr. Kraft spoke at these conferences and invited me to attend and help with the ministry time over multiple years. Later, I enrolled in WLI, where I was introduced to many new friends and associates, with whom more doors to ministry were opened. One new friend, Heather (not her real name), invited me to speak at a spiritual networking conference in South Carolina.

About the time I started doing ministries internationally and I had episodes of falling, literally. It seems like on most trips, I experienced a fall. It started on my first trip to Habsburg, Switzerland, but continued for several years. I did not understand it and felt like I was cursed with it. Every time I was supposed to be on a stage to speak, I had a fear of falling. That fear of falling was finally broken during my ministry trip (pun intended!) to South Carolina with Heather.

The night before I was to speak, I had a dream about falling. When I got to the facility, I noted a tall platform stage. I didn't want to speak from the stage, but being of short stature, people in the back of the auditorium complained they could not see me. So, I got up and spoke from the platform. While speaking on the topic of inner children, one of the attendees had some questions and concerns. In due course, I took a step back and felt something grab the back of my legs, and I froze momentarily thinking that I might fall, and suddenly I found myself flying backward off the platform. My wig flew one way, my shoes fell in two different directions, and I was momentarily bottoms-up with my derrière facing the audience! My host Heather was mortified and jumped onto the stage, looking for my wig and shoes and trying to subtly recover my dignity. I'm sure it was a glorious sight to behold! As I had been putting into practice the four keys to hearing God's voice, in the middle of my predicament, I quieted myself, set my eyes upon Jesus (Jesus, where are you?) and listened for His voice (couldn't journal for obvious reasons, but three out of four is not bad). The first thought I had was *Jesus is under the platform hiding. He is too embarrassed to come out. OK, that was not Jesus.* So, again I quieted my thoughts, looked for Jesus, and intently listened and heard His voice calmly: "Get yourself up and straighten yourself out because these things happen, and you're going to handle yourself graciously." Heather found my wig and one of my shoes. The pastor asked if I would like to take a break to recompose myself, but I adjusted my wig and told them I was good to continue even with one shoe still missing.

I finished my segment and was able to take a break in the pastor's office. I looked at myself in the mirror and noticed that my wig was on backward! Then his phone rang in the office. I didn't answer at first, but it just kept on ringing, so I finally picked it up. There was a man on the other side asking if the conference was still on for the evening and if the lady on the stage who "fell off the platform and lost her hair" was going to be speaking. I replied, "yes" on both counts. The man said he thought that he would really benefit from the teaching based upon what he had heard. Two weeks later, this same man called and left me a message asking for "the lady who fell off the stage and lost her hair" on my answering machine. Weeping, he said he was really hurting and thought that I could help him. He left me his phone number, and I called him back. This man was suicidal and needed immediate help. I was able to "talk him off the ledge" and get him the help he needed through Heather's network resources. I recognized that my fall and the loss of my wig were worth it if it helped this man remember me to be able to get the help he needed.

That was not the only interesting part of that evening session. Earlier that evening, I met a little grandma who was a member of the intercessor team. Before the meeting, she asked if there was anything they could be praying over me for. I said yes and told her to pray for my feet because I have a fear of falling. At the end of the meeting, she asked me if I wanted to know what she saw when I fell. Resisting my natural tendency for a snarky response, I politely replied, "yes." This little grandma told me she saw something push me, but then she heard a noise from the back and saw a large angel rushing from the back of the church, and he leaped across the platform and grabbed the back of my head and neck to either prevent or maybe heal injuries. When we reviewed the tape of the evening, we saw a violent fall and heard a snap that could have been from my neck or head, but I did not feel a thing. Although I felt something about my feet, I did not feel a push, but when I viewed the tape, the fall looked as if I were pushed. It was a miracle that I was not injured. Reflecting upon the evening, my fear of falling was broken. I saw God's grace and His hand of protection upon me from the beginning of the evening through the end. I am not afraid of getting up on a stage. I'm not afraid of embarrassing myself or my ministry partners. That evening, we also received the largest offering we had ever received.

Today I look back on the events of that evening and I laugh. I have come to recognize that not only was my fear of falling broken that evening, but shame also has no hold on me. I do not fear shame. And spirits of deception that tell me that I am a failure, unworthy, or whatever they may say, no longer have a hold on me. I recognize that God uses me for His glory through my weaknesses and failures. In this, I join the Apostle Paul in saying, "My grace is sufficient for you, for My power is perfected in weakness." Therefore I will boast all the more gladly in my weaknesses, so that the power of Christ may rest on me. (2 Cor 12:9)

Reflections of the Heart

I think some of the strongest spiritual forces of evil that you will contend against are the spirits of fear, shame, and deception. Shame and deception are attacks on your identity and can keep you from finding your true self. The spirits of fear are often partnered with shame, and it's the fear of shame that can keep you from walking in the noble purpose that God intends for you unless you recognize their existence and their tactics. The spirits of shame and deception try to keep you from finding your identity in Jesus by telling you how unworthy and unacceptable you are. They are attacks on your character and tell you not to let anyone see the real you. Shame is subtle and typically speaks in the first person and says: "I can't let anyone (especially Jesus) see the real me because I know that they (and He) will reject me. I know if they see my heart, the impurities, perversion, and false motives, I will be judged and condemned." Shame will keep you from receiving Jesus' healing if you let it.

I think it is really important to understand the difference between guilt and shame. Dr. Kraft used to say, "Shame shames you for who you are, but guilt guilts you for what you've done." When guilt is a conviction in your heart of wrongdoing, it is normal and healthy if you process and handle it appropriately. When the Holy Spirit brings a conviction of a sinful act that results in repentance, it is a "healthy guilt." But there are unhealthy forms of guilt. When a demonic spirit of deception condemns you of a sinful act, it turns a healthy guilt toxic. Deceptive spirits take the sinful act and pronounce judgment against your character. These spirits speak to you typically in the first person and say: "I am not good; I am unworthy, unacceptable, perverted, evil . . . I am a sinner!" Deceptive spirits take advantage of our lack of knowledge and twist truths into lies. As long as we live, we are tied to our physical body. That physical body is where sin lives, so to say "I am a sinner" is a truthful statement. But Jesus did not come to redeem our physical bodies. The curse over our bodies is not broken; it is tied to the material world and still undergoes decay day by day until we draw our last breath. Jesus does not look at our physical body when He sees us. It has no eternal value for Him. He did not die for our body or outer person; He died to redeem the inner person. Jesus sees and cares about our hearts. Jesus invites us to see ourselves as He sees us—from the inside. When we fix our eyes upon Jesus, He restores our soul and helps us see ourselves for what we are becoming—and we are becoming more like Him.

Deceptive spirits want us to focus away from Jesus. They want us to see ourselves through the lens of our world culture. It takes the conviction of sin and turns it into a condemnation of character. It takes a healthy guilt and turns it into shame if we let it. If we come into agreement with what shame and deception say we are, then we will view the world and all the people in it through the lenses of shame, deception, and fear. Everyone is evil; everyone lies; everyone cheats. Trust no one!

I share this story because life happens. Shame and deception still try to regain their foothold on me, but I won't let them. I know the enemy's tactics. I know that in every situation, Jesus is always with me. I am not the person I once was, hiding my nervous disorder out of shame. I am not the person who lived in constant fear, trying to manipulate and control everyone and everything around me. Instead of hiding, I have learned to call upon Jesus, knowing that He is always there for me. I can tell you this story and laugh alongside you. I have to admit, God has a sense of humor! I remember the mortified look on Heather's face as she crawled along the floor on her hands and knees, looking for my shoes and wig. I can only imagine what the folks in that auditorium thought as I picked myself up off the floor, wig firmly in place, backward, and continued my talk. How awkward they all must have felt, wondering if they should tell me. How funny would it have been if someone had been brave enough to stop my talk, raise their hand, and say, "Excuse me, Judy, but I think you have your wig on backward!" The thought amuses me and makes me laugh. And then the phone call from a stranger who heard about the lady who fell off the stage, the images of angels protecting me and keeping me from physical harm, and lastly the largest single donation in the history of that conference—wow! When I think about this incident, I am overwhelmed by how God can change what the enemy surely had planned for defeat into a momentous victory. Life happens, but Jesus overcomes.

*   *   *

As you reflect on your own life, have you heard the voices of fear, shame, and deception? What have they been saying to you? Have you come to any agreements with the spirits of deception?

*   *   *

If you know that fear, shame, and deception have ruled over you, examine yourself with the Holy Spirit counsel and guidance. Take a moment to renounce any lies of the enemy that you may have come into agreement with. Renounce any oaths, vows, and/or dedications made as a result of these agreements. Take authority over these spirits and cast them at the feet of Jesus, then ask the Holy Spirit to bring you His peace and freedom.

Two things that have really helped me to become fit for His purposes are the inner healing and deliverance from Dr. Charles Kraft (although I received personal ministry from him, he has authored many books that are invaluable resources - Kraft, Charles. 2010. *Deep Wounds, Deep Healing*, Chosen Books: Bloomington, Minnesota; Kraft, Charles. 2012. *I Give You Authority*, Chosen Books: Bloomington, Minnesota; Kraft, Charles. 2010. *Two Hours to Freedom*, Chosen Books: Bloomington, Minnesota) and learning how to hear God's voice from Mark Virkler (Virkler, Mark. 2010. *4 Keys to Hearing God's Voice*. Destiny Image Publishers: Shippensburg, PA). I have attached references in the bibliography from both these remarkable men of God and highly recommend them to you.

Chapter 14

GOD! - the God of Redemption

Luke 7:36–48

36 One of the Pharisees asked Jesus to eat with him, so Jesus went into the Pharisee's house and sat at the table. 37 A sinful woman in the town learned that Jesus was eating at the Pharisee's house. So she brought an alabaster jar of perfume 38 and stood behind Jesus at his feet, crying. She began to wash his feet with her tears, and she dried them with her hair, kissing them many times and rubbing them with the perfume. 39 When the Pharisee who asked Jesus to come to his house saw this, he thought to himself, "If Jesus were a prophet, he would know that the woman touching him is a sinner!" 40 Jesus said to the Pharisee, "Simon, I have something to say to you." Simon said, "Teacher, tell me." 41 Jesus said, "Two people owed money to the same banker. One owed five hundred coins and the other owed fifty. 42 They had no money to pay what they owed, but the banker told both of them they did not have to pay him. Which person will love the banker more?" 43 Simon, the Pharisee, answered, "I think it would be the one who owed him the most money." Jesus said to Simon, "You are right." 44 Then

Jesus turned toward the woman and said to Simon, "Do you see this woman? When I came into your house, you gave me no water for my feet, but she washed my feet with her tears and dried them with her hair. [45] You gave me no kiss of greeting, but she has been kissing my feet since I came in. [46] You did not put oil on my head, but she poured perfume on my feet. [47] I tell you that her many sins are forgiven, so she showed great love. But the person who is forgiven only a little will love only a little." [48] Then Jesus said to her, "Your sins are forgiven."

I would like to end my story with Luke's recounting of the woman who washed Jesus' feet with her tears and dried them with her hair. This is the woman who had suffered much, and in the depth of her suffering, Jesus found her and restored to her what had been lost and could not be replaced by anyone or anything. She lost her identity and her self-worth; she was an outcast, a sinner in the eyes of her community. She was without hope until Jesus met her. Whatever drove her to the depths of her situation—to the place where sin was her master—was broken. Jesus reached down to lift her out of the pit of her despair, and with the forgiveness of her sins, He set her free.

As I consider this woman in her relationship with Jesus, I believe that there isn't anything she would not do if Jesus asked her. Would she forgive those who used and abused her, judged her, and condemned her? I think the answer is yes. I believe she would do anything Jesus asked of her because she has received much. Unlike Simon the pharisee in this story, who had not received much because he didn't think he needed anything, this woman knew her situation and was able to receive the depth of the grace Jesus had for her, and her response was extravagant! Her extravagant response was a visible demonstration of the depth of wholeness and healing she received in her heart.

I do not know the events and circumstances that led this woman into her depths of despair and sin, but I know she suffered much. I do not compare myself with her, but I know that I do share in her suffering. That we have in common. And just as Jesus reached down and pulled her out of the depth of her despair, Jesus pulled me out of the dumpster that had been my life. Hopelessly broken, He put me back together piece by piece. To this day, He still redeems me.

As I was reviewing and editing the contents of this book, certain memories still caused negative emotions to surface. I mentioned the song "I can't live without you" by Harry Nilsson as having a particularly stirring effect on me—yet God redeemed that song for me. I can listen to it now without the PTSD associated with Danuwoa and our Russian roulette episode. I hear the song and think, *I can't live if living is without you, God.* God redeems, piece by piece, layer by layer, as long as we let Him into those areas we are hurting.

I think that when God asks us to do something impossible, it's only because we have not yet recognized the depth of grace He has already given us. Once we recognize how far down Jesus' reach is and we embrace everything He has to give, then, like the woman in Luke's story who loved much, we too can exhibit extravagant love. Can we turn the other cheek, love our enemies, and pray for those who persecute us (Matt 5:38–48)? The answer is yes, but only when we have received the love, grace, and forgiveness of Jesus. When our inner person has been healed of the wounds and we are made whole, then Jesus' love can manifest through us in ways that are unimaginable.

I know that I am still a work in progress. But I do recognize that Jesus has brought me a long way. I love Charles Kraft dearly and have been doing ministry with him for over twenty-five years, but he is a left-brained academic, and I am the polar opposite. He jokingly describes himself as "semi-charismatic" (he demonstrates this by lifting his hands, palms up halfway, i.e., waist level), whereas I am all in, arms lifted up, shouting my best Pentecostal hallelujahs! Watching us worship side by side can be quite entertaining! I say this because at times our personalities clash. Dr. Kraft has a dry sense of humor, and at times his humor has a bite to it (I am glad he feels safe and familiar enough with me to make a joke, but sometimes it feels insensitive from my perspective). If I had not received the depth of healing in my heart, there would have been many times I would have been deeply injured, but I am not that wounded reactionary person any longer. I would also have to admit that at times during our relationship, I would deliberately say something that was hurtful to him to force him to reject and abandon me. He never wavered and walked with me through my healing process.

Have I moved past that to the point where I can love and pray for people who persecute me? I can honestly say that I am getting there.

I wish I could tell you that God has redeemed everything in my life worth redeeming, but sadly, that is not the case. There are still some areas of my life where I am still waiting upon God, but I do so with hope. I long to have my relationship with Charla restored and redeemed. My heart still aches for her, but I will continue to trust in God that he will redeem my relationship with her for His glory, and I look forward to that day!

Reflections of the Heart

I do not know what happened to this woman who washed Jesus' feet with her tears and dried His feet with her hair. Scriptures do not tell of her beyond this incident, but I suspect that her response was much like mine. Once your broken heart has been made whole and you have been consumed by His overwhelming love, you cannot help but want to be a part of Jesus' mission: to give to others what you have received, to know the freedom, joy, and peace that come from the indwelling of the Holy Spirit in your heart, to heal the brokenhearted and open the eyes of the blind, to love your neighbor as yourself.

For me, loving myself was impossible, yet through my healing process, I have come to love, accept, and forgive myself without conditions. And so now I can love and accept others without conditions and without judgment. I can freely forgive as I have been forgiven. Jesus has given me a purpose for living, and my prayer is that you will find a purpose for your life as you follow in the steps of our loving Lord and Savior, Jesus Christ.

Epilogue

I WOULD LIKE TO ADDRESS ONE LAST THOUGHT THAT I'M SURE many of you have. Maybe you would say to me: "Well, all you have said is good, but what about when you come off your "spiritual high" and back to reality? Back to where the enemy continues to hammer and hammer at you. Tell me again then, how great of a miracle you have experienced in your life."

My answer to you is this! I know that life happens, and the enemy has and will continue to pull every trick he can to derail me. Writing this book has caused me to work through each memory and experience I have had. I had to contend with anger, bitterness, resentment, and unforgiveness. I can honestly say that the spiritual forces of evil behind these emotions do not have a hold on me. But that is not to say that I do not have to contend with them when life happens. One thing that Dr. Kraft stressed in his seminars and in his books is the ability that we have as believers to speak to situations and, if it is an attack of the enemy, to just say, "IF THIS IS THE ENEMY, STOP IT." I have found this to be so true and effective, but unfortunately, some of my situations are not related to an enemy attack directly on me but on those that I care about.

Some years ago, I was faced with a horrible situation. Charles had a close friend, Paul. Paul had been like a dad to Charles, and he had become very close to our family. Paul was always there for us whenever we needed help, especially in times we were struggling financially. One morning, we received a call that Paul had taken a gun to his head. He shot himself in the back of the head, but he was still alive. I went to the hospital to see him.

Here lay a man who extended so much love and compassion to those who deserved it the least. As I laid my hands on him and prayed, I was reminded of the day I stood in the hospital and laid my hands on my dad. The enemy had again managed to bring back many emotional memories. Up until that point, I had not prayed for anyone in the hospital who wasn't family. Paul hadn't accepted the Lord, and I felt compelled to pray for him. That day and till this day, I am determined to stand stronger than ever before. I am determined to walk a life that is pleasing to Father. I am taking a stand against the enemy! I refuse to lose another friend, family member, or acquaintance that Father puts in my pathway, to the enemy!

That day reminded me of just what I have been writing in this book. You never know what is happening in a person's life—their mind, emotions, memories, or body. Just because you think you know them or even live with them doesn't mean you understand them. You are walking in dangerous territory if you are judging them. Only God knows their hearts and motives. Paul had everything to live for, yet he felt he had nothing to live for. Paul died at 3:30 p.m., and he went into eternity without a personal relationship with Jesus. I left that hospital and came straight home and got on my knees before Jesus. I cried out for forgiveness for not being able to detect something so wrong within a friend we loved so dearly. I asked Jesus to give me His heart of love and compassion for His lost and dying children. I asked the Holy Spirit to cause my spirit to become so sensitive that I cannot rest unless Father is at rest. So, my long answer to you is yes, I have come off a "spiritual high" and had to face life and its difficult reality! Yet, the peace and love of God still consume me and give me a desire to see others like myself set free!

My prayer for all who read this and all who hear my testimony is that you come to know the delivering power of God, available to you through the ministry of "inner healing." I pray that the eyes of your heart are opened to see and your ears are opened to hear what the Holy Spirit is showing you and that you begin to seek the things of God for your own life. We may value our traditions, but may you also be open to the things the Holy Spirit is trying to show you, things that might stretch your denominational boundaries beyond their traditional doctrines. May you embrace what the good Holy Spirit shows and be open to the changes that God is bringing into your life.

So, if you were to ask me today, "Do you believe a Christian can be demon-possessed?" my answer is still "NO! Where the Spirit of God dwells, evil cannot dwell." If you asked me, "Can a 'Christian' be demonized?" my answer is, "Absolutely!" I know because I have experienced this in my own life. The best way I know to describe it is this: I had a little dog named Lucy. In the summer, she insists on running through the weeds and grass. Nothing you can say or do will stop her. Unfortunately, this opens her up to her enemy's territory of ticks and fleas.

When Lucy comes into the house, she is still the dachshund she was created to be, but now she has fleas and sometimes a tick or two. It doesn't mean she is any less of a dachshund, but she has enemies attached to her, bringing her discomfort and irritation. If it is a tick, she needs a human to get it off. If it isn't removed, it will just dig its roots deeper and deeper, causing her more pain and torment. She isn't capable of getting it off. We have to remove it so she will be free of ticks and their influence. If she has fleas, she tries to get them, but they just keep jumping around all over her, and she is constantly tormented by them. She needs a human to deal with the fleas by administering flea repellent. Now the best solution would be to keep her from getting into the enemy's territory, but unfortunately, when I open the door, off she goes, getting herself into trouble and coming back to me for relief.

Please know that I am not trying to compare a dog to a human being. I use this simply as an analogy to help you understand the difference between being "possessed" and "having" a demon. Lucy is not possessed by ticks and fleas; she just has them, and in a like manner, Christians are not "possessed" by demonic spirits, but we can have attachments (see Appendix A).

There are times that we get into areas of sin, such as bitterness and unforgiveness, in which we open the door to the enemy's attack, and by doing so, demons are allowed to attach themselves to our flesh, our mind, our emotions, and our memories. In the spirit realm, this is how the enemy gains a "legal right" to form an attachment. We need "Jesus," our healer and deliverer, to set us free from these influences. The Holy Spirit lives within our spirits, but many times, we have not yet given Him total control over every area of our lives. There are areas such as our memories, our emotions, and sometimes our own flesh where we have not yielded. It doesn't mean that we aren't "Christians" or that we don't love God. It doesn't mean we are not saved. It doesn't even mean that we are involved in some terrible, sinful action. It just means that a door has been opened for the enemy to attach themselves to us, and we need Jesus to help us get rid of them.

As I bring this writing to a close, there are a few things that I would like to highlight but leave open-ended. Although some mysteries of the invisible realm have been revealed though my experiences, so much of it is still cloaked in mystery.

I spoke of the Ouija Board and how overwhelmed my dad had become with it. It was only a few months later that my dad began to have migraine headaches. I believe my dad became demonized at this time. Could he have been influenced by demons to make sexual advances toward me? Are there occult demons working with demons of inheritance coming down through the family line that "persuaded" my dad to behave in this aberrant manner? Perhaps his mind had been blocked and he could not remember or admit his sexual advances, or perhaps there was a spirit of deceit there to keep him from admitting it.

It wasn't until I first became so upset with my mother that my throat began to close. Was this the spirit of death trying to kill me (one out of the twenty-five times)? What about the times I had hands put around my throat, trying to choke me? What about all the other times my throat closed? Was this again the spirit of death? I'm sure some of you reading this will say, "It's all just psychological." But I do not believe everything is binary, black or white, or all just psychological. It is not a case of either or, but some portion of both. If you have an emotional issue, you very likely have a demonic attachment as well. Remember that you cannot heal, counsel, or reason with a demonic spirit, and you can only heal a broken heart—it cannot be cast out. As far as my throat closing, it has not closed one time since Dr. Kraft laid his hand on my throat and commanded the spirit of death to release me.

Why have traumatic events always happened on my birthday or anniversary? Had this been the strategy of the enemy to try to convince me that everything had been my fault and that everyone would have been better off if I hadn't been born?

Also, my dad was raised by five aunts, four of whom had diabetes, and my grandmother died as a result of diabetes. I'm sure science tells us that we have a genetic disposition toward certain illnesses, but is there a spiritual component to this? If we break generational curses, can we end the disposition toward these illnesses?

What about the spirit of sexual perversion? I felt so guilty because I was having these sexual dreams—remember how the spirit of sexual perversion said he had tried to get a hook in me but never could get me to sin? My faith was too strong because I always talked to my best friend, the Holy Spirit. Does this not testify of His protection that my grandparents had prayed over me during my childhood? Remember how the enemy spirits had said it could not cross the bloodline (because my grandparents prayed the blood of Jesus over me)?

What about my marriage to Charles? I have always been aware of the power of spoken words. Did I curse him and our marriage? Instead of speaking life into him, our marriage, and our family, did I not speak death instead? I always accused him of lying to me, even when he was being truthful. Is there a spirit of lying that I spoke over him?

Charles was a diesel mechanic, and he also did auto body repair. When he came home from work, I would meet him at the door, demanding he shower right then. Some evenings, I didn't even give him time to get in the house and take his shoes off. I'm sure he felt like I was incessantly nagging him. I think it was the memories of Jim that I had been wrestling with—Jim and his glue and paint abuse. I still distinctly remember the night the medics took him to the hospital and how I was so ashamed and embarrassed that I had ever been married to him because he was so dirty and smelled so bad! Were their demons attached to those memories that caused me to react to Charles, or was it all psychological?

Just before I sent this manuscript over for final edits, Charles perished in an accidental home fire. Charles may have had many faults, but he could be heroic when he needed to be, and he was in this situation. With the house ablaze, he managed to ensure that his wife escaped, but ultimately, he was not able to extricate himself. While I regret the failure of my relationship with Charles, my children will remember him as a valiant hero for his final courageous act.

What about my daughter? I took her car away from her, making her extremely angry with me. What about my feelings when my dad took my car away from me after Mom insisted upon it? As much as I tried to not repeat the mistakes my mother made with me, my relationship with Charla seemed to repeat the same behavioral patterns. Remember the slap? Is there a generational curse against my maternal family line that causes this repeated pattern?

I just bring these questions to your attention for you to realize that we are very complicated people. I encourage you to pray and ask the Holy Spirit to reveal to you why you act and react the way you do to both negative and positive thoughts and circumstances in your life. The Holy Spirit has really been able to administer deep healing to my memories. Negative emotional thoughts and attitudes no longer have any control over my life. I am now able to walk in the peace of God, not reacting with the emotions within my memories, but by reacting with love, peace, and forgiveness as the Holy Spirit directs.

As I began to write this testimony, I prayed, "Father, I don't know why You are directing me to expose events in my life and expose something so embarrassing as trichotillomania. People will never understand how anyone could reach a place where they would pull out their own hair." But with a little research, I found that there are five to ten million Americans affected by this compulsive disorder. Did this expose one of the enemy's lies he had been telling me? "Don't share this with anyone. After all, no one pulls their own hair out!" Psychologists will tell you that you cannot be cured of compulsive disorders, but now I recognize there are demonic aspects to them. I know that I do not have the compulsion to pull my hair out ever since Jesus healed me. For my readers, if you have a compulsive disorder, pray about whether there is a demonic attachment to it and ask God to take it away. If needed, look for someone who has experience with inner healing and deliverance and ask them to pray for you to heal the source or root. Today, when I hear someone joking around and saying, "I'm so mad or frustrated that I could pull my hair out!" I'm not so quick to laugh. They very well may be serious!

Shortly after I had started speaking out openly about my trichotillomania, I had four people approach me. They usually are very quiet and reserved, but they start out by saying, "I have a relative or a friend who pulls at their hair. I thought they were the only ones who did this, but after hearing your testimony and understanding why they are doing this, I am able to better understand them and realize maybe they aren't insane but just may have a broken heart! Can you tell me how to help them?" My answer is always the same! The answer is Jesus and "spiritual warfare" done in conjunction with inner healing! They have to come to the place where they realize they were created by God to be just the person they are. Healing came to me when I realized I am who God created me to be, and that is what is important.

I want to be a witness like Proverbs 14:25 (Amplified) speaks of: "A true witness saves lives, but a deceitful witness speaks lies [and endangers lives]." I no longer want to be a "deceitful witness," pretending to be someone other than the person God created me to be. I want to be a "true witness that saves lives"! God has miraculously changed my life. The attitudes and desires I now have and aspire to grow stronger in are these:

1. May I always remember that when nothing else works, the unconditional love of God can and will penetrate the hardest of hearts.

2. His love covers a multitude of sins. Without His love flowing through our lives, we are worthless to Jesus and His church.

3. May I never be quick to judge others; I don't know what is going on in their lives.

4. May each conversation I have be led by the Holy Spirit so that I may be sensitive to the hurts and pain of the other person's heart.

5. May the Holy Spirit guard me from being used by the enemy to administer that last blow to a person's low self-esteem. That person may be hanging in the balance of a decision, trying to decide if their life is even worth living. They may be trying desperately to convince themselves that they do have a purpose in life.

6. May I always be used as a noble vessel of God through which His unconditional love and acceptance flow.

7. May my testimony always be of the healing power of Father God and of the precious blood of Jesus, our resurrection Christ.

8. May I speak the life of God to a person who is without God.

9. May my testimony, by the power of the Holy Spirit, speak:

    a. Life to those who feel they are dead.
    b. Freedom to those who are bound by the enemy.
    c. Peace to those who are in constant torment by the enemy.
    d. Hope to those who have no hope.
    e. Love to those who have no love or are unlovable.

10. May my testimony, by the power of the Holy Spirit, bring a desire for:

    a. More of the things of God.
    b. More intimate relationship with Jesus.
    c. More true fellowship with the Holy Spirit.

11. May I always be reminded that Jesus isn't looking for me to be perfect. I just have be me—the true me.

I invite you to become a member of the "body of Christ" that the Holy Spirit can use as a noble vessel, in which the "healing balm of Gilead" may be applied to the deepest, innermost hurts within the hearts of God's children.

Appendix A

Can Christians be demonized?

By Robert Morita

THERE ARE MULTIPLE EXCELLENT REFERENCES ON THIS SUBJECT matter. I have referenced two of my favorite authors on this matter, Dr. Charles Kraft (Kraft, Charles. 2012. *I Give You Authority*, Chosen Books: Bloomington, Minnesota; Kraft, Charles. 2010. *Two Hours to Freedom*, Chosen Books: Bloomington, Minnesota; Kraft, Charles. 2015. *The Evangelical's Guide to Spiritual Warfare*, Chosen Books: Bloomington, Minnesota) and Dr. Neal Anderson (Anderson, Neal. 2019. *Bondage Breakers*, Harvest House Publishers: Eugene, Oregon; Anderson, Neal. 2014. *Victory over Darkness*, Bethany House Publishers: Minneapolis, Minnesota) in the bibliography. I do have my own opinions, most certainly influenced by these and other writers, but also based upon my experiences in inner healing and deliverance prayers and in my own scripture study.

As noted by many theologians, the term "demon-possessed" is a poor interpretation of the original language. A better interpretation would be "has a demon," "demonized," or "demonic attachment" (see references in the bibliography for more information). My intent is to explain this to the layperson involved in inner healing and deliverance ministry in non-theological terms without missing the deeper understanding needed for what is still a mystery into the invisible spiritual realm.

I will use the term "demonized" as this has become the popular choice, at least in the books I have read. Possession is not a suitable interpretation because it connotes ownership, and demons cannot "own" a human soul. There is always a matter of choice; we choose what "voices" to follow. Now to be clear, the voices I am referring to are not audible sounds you would hear as if someone were speaking to you (which is really nothing more than vibrating airwaves hitting your eardrum). It is the quiet or sometimes not so quiet inner voices or thoughts we all hear all the time. Some people refer to it as "self-talk." In the secular world, all self-talk is simply originated by your own mind and imagination. I propose that your imagination is much more sophisticated than secularists have understood it to be (even though everyone will admit that the imagination is something that even the most brilliant minds are not able to replicate in their studies of artificial intelligence). I chose to use the term "sanctified imagination," which I first understood from the works of Dr. Leann Payne (Payne, Leeanne. 1996. *The Broken Image*, Hamewith Books: Grand Rapids, Michigan; Payne, Leeanne. 1996. *Restoring the Christian Soul*, Hamewith Books: Grand Rapids, Michigan; Payne, Leeanne. 1995. *The Healing Presence*, Hamewith Books: Grand Rapids, Michigan). She generally used the term "True Imagination" in her writing. Sanctified imagination is simply using the ability that God created in you to see or hear things that are real but invisible. But if your imagination can be used for sanctified purposes, it can be used for unsanctified purposes. Lustful or arrogant self-promoting thoughts may come from your own sinful cravings in your flesh, but I also propose that some thoughts may originate not from yourself or the Holy Spirit but from spiritual forces of evil in the heavenly realms (Eph 6:10–20). We all have to put on the full armor of God to withstand the attacks of the enemy, but when the enemy has a right to be attached to our souls, and if we are not even aware of this, then we can unwittingly be used by the enemy to serve his purposes. We must always be aware of the enemy's tactics (2 Cor 2:11). For those who believe that a demonic attachment for a Christian is not biblical, I give you 2 Cor 12:5–10. This is the verse regarding Paul's infamous "thorn in the flesh." While this is a much-debated verse, look at it simply without trying to force your theology to fit. This "thorn" is described as a messenger of Satan. Paul asked that "it" be taken away from him; note that if this were an illness, Paul most likely would have said "three times I asked the Lord to heal me" or something like that. The text does not amend itself to a physical ailment. This was a tormenting spirit, and there is biblical precedent for this kind of tormenting spirit (see 1 Sam 16:14). Jesus tells us a parable of folks who would be subject to torment if they did not forgive as they have been forgiven (Matt 18:21–35). Paul's situation was unique. It is not an issue of unforgiveness, but God allowed a tormenting spirit to keep Paul humble. Fortunately for us, the apostle Paul was a special case. We are given the authority to rebuke and cast-off demonic attachments from us as long as we have removed the rights that the demons have for their attachment. For more on this, read the aforementioned books listed in the bibliography. There is one more point regarding this "thorn in the flesh." Biblically speaking, the flesh is sometimes noted as the physical body, and at other times it refers to the carnal self, which is the body but may also include some portion of our soul. The important distinction I am making here is that it is not our spirit. When we say "yes" to Jesus, our spirit and the Holy Spirit are conjoined to form a new creation (2 Cor 5:17). However, it is important to note that we are made up of three parts: a physical body, the soul (mind, will, and emotions), and a spirit. It is the spirit that is made new, most certainly not the physical body. This physical body continues its process of decay and eventually will stop to function, i.e., the body dies. The soul is eternal, but it is not immediately changed. We will carry our mind, memories, and will into eternity. Once we have a new spirit, the soul is transformed as long as we submit to the Holy Spirit and not our carnal self or the "flesh." For more on this topic, I invite you to read three books by Phil Mason (Mason, Phil. 2013. *The Heart Journey*, Independently published; Mason, Phil. 2015. *The Knowledge of the Heart*, Independently published; Mason, Phil. 2015. *The New Creation Miracle*, Independently published). This transformation of our soul or heart is what we call inner healing.

Appendix B

How much power do demons have?

By Robert Morita

THOUGH THE CHRISTIAN CHURCH MOST CERTAINLY ACKNOWL-EDGES THE EXISTENCE OF ANGELS AND DEMONS, IN THE Western Church there is very little teaching regarding spiritual warfare. Furthermore, in the vacuum of sound knowledge, humanity fills in the blanks based upon fear, hearsay, and myth. In this void, opinions regarding demonic power tend toward the extremes. Either Satan is the evil power, the rival of the Almighty God and is a being to be feared and left alone (unless you are a professional exorcist) or Satan and the entire demonic realm are a myth. I posit that both extremes are inaccurate.

First off, Satan is real but invisible. If you believe that the Bible is the word of God (as I do), then you have to accept the reality of Satan, demons, angels, and the whole invisible realm. There are a multitude of books written on this subject, some of which I mentioned in Appendix A, but for this particular subject, I would add *The Evangelical's Guide to Spiritual Warfare* by Charles Kraft (Kraft, Charles. 2015. *The Evangelical's Guide to Spiritual Warfare*, Chosen Books: Bloomington, Minnesota) and *Spiritual Warfare* by Ray Stedman (Stedman, Ray. 1999. *Spiritual Warfare*, Discovery House Publishers: Grand Rapids, Michigan).

A brief Biblical view of Satan is summarized herein:

- Satan is a created being and therefore not equivalent to God (Eze 28:11–17).
- Satan's rival is not God but the archangel Michael (Jude 9).
- In contending against Satan, Michael yields to God in rebuking him (Jude 9).
- God limits Satan's power and authority (Job) with respect to his influence on humanity.
- Satan has been given authority over the kingdoms of this world (Matt 4:8–9).
- Demonic beings have ranking and authority over regions and kingdoms of this world (Dan. 10; Eph 6:12).

Our ability to resist the devil (James 4:7) and authority to cast out demons (Matt 10:1,8) come from Jesus. We have the authority, but only in submission to Jesus. Following Jesus' lead, we do only as we "see" and "hear" as His Holy Spirit leads. To go beyond his provision is unwise. Like the archangel Michael, we should ask Jesus to rebuke Satan if we find ourselves in a place outside the boundaries of our authority. However, within the boundaries of our authority (this would include our place of residence, workplace, neighbor, church we attend, and normal places where we go for work and socialization but not places dedicated for evil practices and/or demonic strongholds), we are commissioned by Jesus and His Holy Spirit to cast off demons (along with other signs and wonders). We do not have to fear retribution from the enemy.

We are called to be a part of his royal priesthood (1 Pet. 2:9), and part of our priestly calling is to cast off unclean spirits. That said, we must always recognize that God grants people free will to choose what they will submit to. We do not have the authority to cast off an unclean spirit from someone who desires to be partnered with one and chooses to submit freely to them.

Outside our area of authority, we are not powerless, but a greater concerted and unified approach by a significant population of those living in and around the affected region is required. For more information on this subject matter, I would invite you to read *The Twilight Labyrinth* and *Informed Intercession* by George Otis Jr. (Otis, George, Jr. 1997. *The Twilight Labyrinth*, Chosen Books: Grand Rapids, Michigan; Otis, George, Jr. 1999. *Informed Intercessor*, Renew Books: Ventura, California)

Appendix C

Inner Child, Dissociative Identity Disorder, and Demonization

REFERENCES CONTAINED IN THIS BOOK REGARDING INNER children and dissociative identity disorder (DID) are made from personal experiences and encounters with folks who cover the spectrum between them. We (Robert Morita and Judy Taber) do not claim to be educated experts and/or trained psychologists in these complex psychological areas and will defer to those that are with respect to clinical definitions and diagnoses of individuals who may believe that they have had experiences that are consistent with the descriptions contained in this book. We are not recommending that anyone reading this book who is under psychological care for DID discontinue receiving appropriate professional care.

All that said, there is additional information that we believe needs to be addressed. In our Western culture, there is a tendency to polarize our belief system. People hold to either a secular western ideology that demons are not real, it is a myth (i.e., religious superstition) or the extreme opposite held by some Christians that demons do exist and are so powerful to the extent of being able control people. We believe that both extremes are in error.

We obviously believe in the existence of demons and that they can influence people—even Christians. But we believe in the science of psychology with respect to dissociative disorder and inner children. Our experience tells us that when someone has a dissociative disorder or an inner child who has experienced trauma, they are highly likely to be demonized. It is not a question of either/or; it is more likely that the person has both. While psychologists may be qualified to handle emotional well-being and healing, without understanding the effect that demonization presents, the path to wholeness and freedom may not be achieved to the degree desired.

Bibliography

Anderson, Neal. 2019. *Bondage Breakers*, Harvest House Publishers: Eugene, Oregon

Anderson, Neal. 2014. *Victory over Darkness*, Bethany House Publishers: Minneapolis, Minnesota

Kraft, Charles. 2010. *Deep Wounds, Deep Healing*, Chosen Books: Bloomington, Minnesota

Kraft, Charles. 2012. *I Give You Authority*, Chosen Books: Bloomington, Minnesota

Kraft, Charles. 2010. *Two Hours to Freedom*, Chosen Books: Bloomington, Minnesota

Kraft, Charles. 2015. *The Evangelical's Guide to Spiritual Warfare*, Chosen Books: Bloomington, Minnesota

Leman, Kevin. 1990. *Growing Up Firstborn*. Dell Publishing: New York, New York

Mason, Phil. 2013. *The Heart Journey*, Independently published

Mason, Phil. 2015. *The Knowledge of the Heart*, Independently published

Mason, Phil. 2015. *The New Creation Miracle*, Independently published

Otis, George, Jr. 1997. *The Twilight Labyrinth*, Chosen Books: Grand Rapids, Michigan

Otis, George, Jr. 1999. *Informed Intercessor*, Renew Books: Ventura, California

Bibliography

Payne, Leeanne. 1996. *The Broken Image*, Hamewith Books: Grand Rapids, Michigan

Payne, Leeanne. 1996. *Restoring the Christian Soul*, Hamewith Books: Grand Rapids, Michigan

Payne, Leeanne. 1995. *The Healing Presence*, Hamewith Books: Grand Rapids, Michigan

Stedman, Ray. 1999. *Spiritual Warfare*, Discovery House Publishers: Grand Rapids, Michigan

Virkler, Mark. 2010. *4 Keys to Hearing God's Voice*. Destiny Image Publishers: Shippensburg, PA